Important Instruction

Use the URL or QR code provided below to unlock all the online learning resources included with this Grade 3 to 4 summer learning activities workbook.

URL	QR Code
Visit the URL below for online registration **http://www.lumoslearning.com/a/tg3-4**	

Your online access includes;

- Skills practice resources for Grade 4 Math and ELA
- Grade-appropriate passages to improve reading skills
- Grade 3 vocabulary quizzes
- Access to Lumos Flashcube - An interactive tool to improve vocabulary
- Educational videos, worksheets, standards information and more

Additional Benefits of Online Registration

- Entry to Lumos Weekly Summer Photo Contest
- Entry to Lumos Short Story Competition

Lumos Learning
Developed by Expert Teachers

Summer Learning HeadStart, Grade 3 to 4: Fun Activities Plus Math, Reading, and Language Workbooks

Contributing Author   - Leigh Hargett
Contributing Author   - Keyana M
Contributing Author   - Julie C. Lyons
Contributing Editor   - George Smith
Contributing Author   - Marisa Adams
Executive Producer   - Mukunda Krishnaswamy

First Edition - 2020

ISBN 10: 1940484693

ISBN 13: 978-1-940484-69-3

Printed in the United States of America

Last updated - April 2022

For permissions and additional information contact us

Lumos Information Services, LLC   Email: support@lumoslearning.com
PO Box 1575, Piscataway, NJ 08855-1575   Tel: (732) 384-0146
http://www.LumosLearning.com   Fax: (866) 283-6471

Developed by Expert Teachers

Table of Contents

Introduction

What is Summer Academic Learning Loss?

What is Summer Academic Learning Loss? Studies show that if students take a standardized test at the end of the school year, and then repeat that test when they return in the fall, they will lose approximately four to six weeks of learning. In other words, they could potentially miss more questions in the fall than they would in the spring. This loss is commonly referred to as the summer slide.

When these standardized testing scores drop an average of one month, it causes teachers to spend at least the first four to five weeks, on average, re-teaching critical material. In terms of math, students typically lose an average of two and a half months of skills, and when reading and math losses are combined, it averages three months; it may even be lower for students in lower-income homes.

And on average, the three areas students will typically lose ground in are spelling, vocabulary, and mathematics.

How can You Help Combat Summer Learning Loss?

Like anything, academics are something that requires practice, and if they are not used regularly, you run the risk of losing them. Because of this, it is imperative your children work to keep their minds sharp over the summer. There are many ways to keep your children engaged over the summer, and we're going to explore some of the most beneficial.

Start with School:

Your best source of information is your child's school. Have a conversation with your child's teacher. Tell them you are interested in working on some academics over the summer and ask what suggestions they might have. Be sure to ask about any areas your child may be struggling in and for a list of books to read over the summer. Also, talk to your child's counselor. They may have recommendations of local summer activities that will relate back to the schools and what your child needs to know. Finally, ask the front office staff for any information on currently existing after school programs (the counselor may also be able to provide this). Although after school programs may end shortly, the organizations running them will often have information on summer camps. Many of these are often free or at a very low cost to you and your family.

Stay Local:

Scour your local area for free or low-cost activities and events. Most museums will have dollar days of some kind where you can get money-off admission for going on a certain day of the week or a certain time. Zoos will often do the same thing. Take lunch to the park and eat outside, talking about the leaves, flowers, or anything else you can find there. Your child can pick one favorite thing and research it. Attend concerts or shows put on by local artists, musicians, or other vendors. There are many other options available; you just have to explore and find them. The key here is to engage your children. Have them look online with you or search the local newspapers/magazines. Allow them to plan the itinerary, or work with you on it, and when they get back, have them write a journal about the activity. Or, even better, have them write a letter or email to a family member about what they did.

Practice Daily:

Whether the choice is a family activity or experiencing the local environment, staying academically focused is the key is to keep your child engaged every day. This daily practice helps keep student's minds sharp and focused, ensuring they will be able to not only retain the knowledge they have learned, but in many cases begin to move ahead for the next year.

Summer Strategies for Students

Summer is here, which brings a time of excitement, relaxation, and fun. School is the last thing on your mind, but that doesn't mean learning has to be on vacation too. In fact, learning is as just as important and be just as fun (if not more) during the summer months than during the school year.

Did you know that during the summer:

- Students often lose an average of 2 and ½ months of math skills
- Students often lose 2 months of reading skills
- Teachers spend at least the first 4 to 5 weeks of the next school year reteaching important skills and concepts

Your brain is like a muscle, and like any muscle, it must be worked out regularly, and like this, your language arts and math skills are something that requires practice; if you do not use them regularly, you run the risk of losing them. So, it is very important you keep working through the summer. But, it doesn't always have to be 'school' type of work. There are many ways to stay engaged, and we're going to spend a little time looking through them.

Read and Write as Often as Possible

Reading is one of the most important things you can do to keep your brain sharp and engaged. Here are some tips to remember about summer reading:

- Often, summer is the perfect time to find and read new books or books you have always been curious about. However, without your teacher, you may struggle with finding a book that is appropriate for your reading level. In this case, you just have to remember the five-finger rule: open a book to a random page and begin reading aloud, holding up one finger for each word you cannot say or do not know. If you have more than five fingers visible, then the book is probably too hard to read.

- Reading goes beyond books; there are so many other ways to read. Magazines are a great way to keep kids connected to learning, and they encourage so many different activities. National Geographic Kids, Ranger Rick, and American Girl are just a few examples. As silly as it may sound, you can also read the backs of cereal boxes and billboards to work on reading confidence and fluency, and learn many new things along the way! And thinking completely outside the box, you can also read when singing karaoke. Reading the words as they flash across the screen is a great way to build fluency. You can also turn the closed captioning on when a TV show is on to encourage literacy and reading fluency.

But writing is equally as important, and there are many things you can do to write over the summer:

- First, consider keeping a journal of your summer activities. You can detail the things you do, places you go, even people you meet. Be sure to include as much description as possible – sights, sounds, colors should all be included so you can easily remember and visualize the images. But the wonderful thing about a journal is that spelling and sentence structure are not as important. It's just the practice of actually writing;   that is where your focus should be. The other nice thing about a journal is that this informal writing is just for you; with journal writing you don't have to worry about anything, you just have to start writing.

- But if you want a little more depth to your journaling, and you want to share it with others, there is a fantastic opportunity for you with blogging. With parental approval, you can create a blog online where you can share your summer experiences with friends, family, or any others. The wonderful thing about blogs is that you can play with the privacy settings and choose whom you want to see your blogs. You can make it private, where only the individuals who you send the link to can see it, or you can choose for it to be public where anyone can read it. Of course, if you are keeping a blog, you will have to make it a little more formal and pay attention to spelling, grammar, and sentences simply because you want to make sure your blog is pleasing to those who are reading it. Some popular places to post blogs are Blogger, Wordpress, Squarespace, and Quillpad.

Practice Math in Real Life

One way you can keep your brain sharp is by looking at the world around you and finding ways to include math. In this case, we're thinking of fun, practical ways to practice in your daily life.

- First, have some fun this summer with being in charge of some family projects. Suggest a fun project to complete with a parent or grandparent; decide on an area to plant some new bushes or maybe a small home project you can work on together. You can help design the project and maybe even research the best plants to plant or the best way to build the project. Then write the shopping list, making sure you determine the correct amount of supplies you will need. Without even realizing it, you would have used some basic math calculations and geometry to complete the project.

- You can also find math in shopping for groceries or while doing some back to school shopping. For each item that goes into the cart, estimate how much it will be and keep a running estimation of the total cost. Make it a competition before you go by estimating what your total bill will be and see who comes the closest. Or, you can even try and compete to see who can determine the correct total amount of tax that will be needed. And a final mental game to play while shopping is to determine the change you should receive when paying with cash. Not only is this a good skill to practice math, more importantly, helps you make sure you're getting the correct change.

- You can even use everyday math if you are doing any traveling this summer, and there are many fun ways to do this. Traveling requires money, and someone has to be in charge of the budget. You can volunteer to be the family accountant. Make a budget for the trip and keep all the receipts. Tally up the cost of the trip and even try to break it up by category – food, fun, hotels, gas are just a few of the categories you can include. For those of you who might be looking for even more of a challenge, you can calculate what percentage of your budget has been spent on each category as well.

- And traveling by car gives many opportunities as well. Use the car odometer to calculate how far you have traveled. For an added challenge, you can see if you can calculate how much gas you used as well as how many gallons of gas per mile have been used.

Practice Daily:

Whether the choice is a family activity or experiencing the local environment, staying academically focused is the key to keep your mind engaged every day. That daily practice keeps your brain sharp and focused, and helps to ensure that you are not only able to retain the knowledge you learned last year but also to get a jump start on next year's success too!

How to Use This Workbook Effectively During Summer

This book offers a variety of state standards aligned resources, in both printed and online format, to help students learn during Summer months.

The activities in the book are organized by week and aligned with the 3rd-grade learning standards. We encourage you to start at the beginning of Summer holidays. During each week, students can complete daily Math and English practice. There are five daily practice worksheets for each week. Students can log in to the online program once a week to complete reading, vocabulary and writing practice. Students can work on fun activity anytime during that week. Additionally, students can record their Summer activity through the online program.

Please note that the online program also includes access to 4th grade learning resources. This section of the online program could be used to help students to get a glimpse of what they would be learning in the next grade level.

Weekly Fun Summer Photo Contest

Take a picture of your summer fun activity and share it on Twitter or Instagram

Use the **#SummerLearning** mention

@LumosLearning on Twitter or

@lumos.learning on Instagram

Tag friends and increase your chances of winning the contest

Participate and stand a chance to WIN $50 Amazon gift card!

Take Advantage of the Online Resources

To access the online resources included with this book, parents and teachers can register with a FREE account. With each free signup, student accounts can be associated to enable online access for them.

Once the registration is complete, the login credentials for the created accounts will be sent in email to the id used during signup. Students can log in to their student accounts to get started with their summer learning. Parents can use the parent portal to keep track of student's progress.

URL	QR Code
Visit the URL below for online registration **http://www.lumoslearning.com/a/tg3-4**	

Lumos Short Story Competition 2022

**Write a Short Story
Based On Your Summer Experiences**

Get A Chance To Win $100 Cash Prize
+
1 Year Free Subscription To Lumos StepUp
+
Trophy With Certificate

How can my child participate in this competition?

Step 1
Visit **www.lumoslearning.com/a/tg3-4** to register for online fun summer program.

Step 2
After registration, your child can upload their summer story by logging into the student portal and clicking on Lumos Short Story Competition 2022.
Last date for submission is August 31, 2022

How is this competition judged?
Lumos teachers will review students submissions in Sep 2022. Quality of submission would be judged based on creativity, coherence and writing skills.

We recommend short stories that are less than 500 words.

Week 1 Summer Practice

Understanding Multiplication (3.OA.A.1)

Day 1

1. Which multiplication fact is being modeled below?

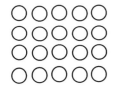

- Ⓐ 3 x 10 = 30
- Ⓑ 4 x 10 = 40
- Ⓒ 4 x 9 = 36
- Ⓓ 3 x 9 = 27

2. Which numerical expression describes this array?

○○○○○
○○○○○
○○○○○
○○○○○

- Ⓐ 4 + 5
- Ⓑ 5 + 4
- Ⓒ 4 x 5
- Ⓓ 4 x 4

3. Which number sentence describes this array?

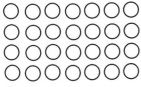

- Ⓐ 8 x 4 = 32
- Ⓑ 7 + 5 = 12
- Ⓒ 5 x 7 = 35
- Ⓓ 7 x 4 = 28

4. Complete the following table:

Number of lions	5	6	9		
Total number of legs	20			32	16

Margaret was a simple lady who lived in a village with her husband, Robert. They had a daughter named Amy. Every day at sunrise, Margaret would wake up, cook, clean, and feed the cattle. Robert would milk the cows and then take the dogs for a long walk. Amy would study, help her mother for some time, and then get ready for school.

Amy studied in a school that was far away from her house, but she loved going to school. She went with her friends, Ingrid and Rebecca. They would walk together chatting, laughing, and singing songs as they went. They had to cross a river on the way. The only way they could cross it was by walking on a narrow bridge.
One day Margaret, Robert, Amy, and her friends were walking on the narrow bridge one behind the other. Amy and her friends were off to school as usual, Margaret and Robert wanted to go to the market on the other side of the river to buy groceries for the house.

As they were crossing the narrow bridge, Rebecca slipped. She gave a frightened scream, clutching Ingrid, who was in front of her. Both of them lost their balance and fell into the river. Amy clutched her mother in fright. For a moment, she hesitated, and then threw herself into the river after her friends, determined to save them.

Margaret screamed, and Robert jumped into the river. Some passers-by also jumped into the river and rescued the children, who were dripping wet, and shivering with fright.

That night Robert patted his daughter Amy and said, "You are a brave girl Amy, I'm proud of you."

5. How is Margaret related to Amy?

(A) She is her cousin.
(B) She is her friend.
(C) She is her mother.
(D) She is her aunt.

6. Who slipped on the narrow bridge?

(A) Amy.
(B) Margaret.
(C) Robert.
(D) Rebecca.

7. Why did Robert and Margaret go along with the girls?

- Ⓐ They wanted to walk them to school.
- Ⓑ They wanted to go for a walk.
- Ⓒ They wanted to buy some groceries.
- Ⓓ They wanted to walk on the bridge.

Eight-year-old Tess heard her parents talking about her little brother Andrew. She realized something was wrong. Andrew was very sick, and they did not have enough money for his treatment. Tess heard her daddy say, "Only a miracle can save him now."

Tess went to her bedroom and retrieved a jar from its hiding place. There were a few coins in it. She counted them carefully. She then made her way to the drug store. The pharmacist was too busy to pay attention to her. "And what do you want?" he asked, annoyed at her persistence. "Can't you see that I am talking to my brother? He is here from Chicago."

Tess persisted, "My brother's really sick …….. and I want to buy a miracle. His name is Andrew. He has something bad growing inside of his head and my daddy says only a miracle can save him now. So, how much does a miracle cost?" Tess rambled.

The pharmacist's brother, a well-dressed man, stooped down and asked the girl. "What kind of miracle does your brother need?"

"Don't know," replied Tess, eyes welling up with tears. "I just know Mommy says he needs an operation. But my daddy can't pay for it. So, I want to use my money."

The man from Chicago asked, "How much money do you have?

"One dollar and eleven cents," said Tess.

"Well, what a coincidence," smiled the man.

"One dollar and eleven cents is the exact price of a miracle for your little brother." He took her money in one hand and grasped Tess's hand in the other. "Take me to where you live. I want to see your brother and meet your parents. Let's see if I have the kind of miracle you need."

The well-dressed man was Carlton Armstrong, a neurosurgeon. He operated on Andrew without charging any money. It wasn't long until Andrew was home and well again. "I wonder how much the surgery cost?" said Mother.

Tess smiled to herself. She knew exactly how much the miracle cost— one dollar and eleven cents…. plus the immense faith of a little child.

8. Why were Tess's parents worried? Circle the correct answer choice.

Ⓐ   They did not know what was wrong with her brother.

Ⓑ   Tess had little money in her piggybank.

Ⓒ   Andrew was sick and they had no money for treatment.

Ⓓ   Tess did not know the price of a miracle.

Challenge Yourself!

- **Understanding Multiplication**
- **The Question Session**

http://www.lumoslearning.com/a/dc3-1

Day 1

See Page 7 for Signup details

Day 2

1. George is canning pears. He has 100 pears and he divides the pears evenly among 10 pots. How many pears does George put in each pot?

Ⓐ 9 pears
Ⓑ 5 pears
Ⓒ 8 pears
Ⓓ 10 pears

2. Marisa made 15 woolen dolls. She gave the same number of woolen dolls to 3 friends. How many dolls did Marisa give to each friend?

Ⓐ 4 woolen dolls
Ⓑ 3 woolen dolls
Ⓒ 5 woolen dolls
Ⓓ 6 woolen dolls

3. Lisa bought 50 mangos. She divided them equally into 5 basins. How many mangos did Lisa put in each basin?

Ⓐ 10 mangos
Ⓑ 8 mangos
Ⓒ 5 mangos
Ⓓ 7 mangos

4. For each expression below, choose the correct symbol to be filled in the blank.

	<	>	=
30 ÷ 5 ____ 42 ÷ 6	○	○	○
72 ÷ 8 ____ 63 ÷ 7	○	○	○
54 ÷ 6 ____ 56 ÷ 7	○	○	○

One day, a baby elephant was happily dancing through the jungle, nodding his head and lifting up his trunk to trumpet loudly.

The loud sound woke up a monkey who was sleeping in a tree nearby. He was very angry. He scolded the elephant and asked him to keep quiet.

"You silly animal," he said. "Can't you keep quiet? I'm sleeping."

"Oh, sorry," said the little elephant and walked on. After some time, the little elephant reached a river and saw some beautiful swans there. He gazed at the beautiful birds. The swans looked at him and began to laugh.

"Oh! Look at that big creature," they said. "What a long nose, his ears are like fans, and look at his skin, it's much too big for him. He looks like a big wrinkled bag with all of those folds!" They laughed at him, and swam away.

The little elephant was very sad. He tried to smooth out his skin with his trunk but it was no good. He thought, "Why am I so ugly? Let me hide so that no one can see me."

He tried to hide in a thick bush but he disturbed some nests. The birds flew above his head crying loudly while trying to peck at him.

The little elephant ran for cover. He went behind a big rock to hide. Suddenly, he saw a big bear coming towards him. It was growling and appeared to be very angry. The little elephant was very frightened and trumpeted loudly. Just as he trumpeted, he heard a loud crashing and stomping. A herd of elephants came charging to the rescue.

Seeing the herd, the frightened bear ran away.

The little elephant joyfully ran to the big elephants, thanked them, and said, "I wish I could be like you. You're so mighty and strong," he continued.

"But you are," replied the elephants. "You're a perfect little elephant." The little elephant danced for joy, he trumpeted loudly, and walked away happily with the other elephants following behind.

5. What caused the monkey to wake up in this story?

Ⓐ The wind was making a loud noise.
Ⓑ The elephant trumpeted loudly.
Ⓒ The monkey fell down.
Ⓓ The monkey was not asleep in the story.

6. Why did the swans laugh at the elephant?

- Ⓐ They thought that the elephant looked ugly.
- Ⓑ The elephant was happy.
- Ⓒ The elephant was looking at them.
- Ⓓ The elephant was dancing.

7. In this story, what caused the bear to run away?

- Ⓐ He didn't want to see the monkey.
- Ⓑ He was tired.
- Ⓒ He was frightened by the herd of elephants.
- Ⓓ He wanted to bring its friends.

FOREIGN LANDS

UP into the cherry tree
Who should climb but little me?
I held the trunk with both my hands
And looked abroad on foreign lands.

I saw the next-door garden lie,
Adorned with flowers, before my eye,
And many pleasant faces more
That I had never seen before.

I saw the dimpling river pass
And be the sky's blue looking-glass;
The dusty roads go up and down
With people tramping in to town.

If I could find a higher tree
Farther and farther I should see,
To where the grown-up river slips
Into the sea among the ships.

To where the roads on either hand
Lead onward into fairy land,
Where all the children dine at five,
And all the playthings come alive.

- By Robert Louis Stevenson

8. Reading poetry can often help you to draw pictures in your mind. Reread the poem again and see if you can draw atleast one picture in your mind. Illustrate (draw) or write about what image or images come to mind when you read this poem."

Challenge Yourself!

- **Understanding Division**
- **Tell Me Again**

http://www.lumoslearning.com/a/dc3-2

See Page 7 for Signup details

Day 2

1. 54 x 3 = ?
   The product in this number sentence is _____.

   (A) 54
   (B) 162
   (C) 3
   (D) 54 and 3

2. The Snack Shop has twice as many popcorn balls as they do cotton candy. If there are 30 popcorn balls, how many cotton candies are there?

   (A) 7
   (B) 450
   (C) 30
   (D) 15

3. Monica has 56 DVDs in her movie collection. This is 8 times as many as Sue has. How many DVDs does Sue have?

   (A) 8
   (B) 6
   (C) 7
   (D) 10

4. There are 48 cupcakes to be shared equally among 6 boys. How many cupcakes will each boy get?

   [_____] Cup Cakes

A thirsty crow found a pitcher with just a little water in the bottom. His long, slender beak could just touch the water, but he could not get a drink. Looking around, the crow noticed many small stones lying nearby. Patiently, he picked up the stones one by one, and filled the pitcher until the water was high enough for him to get a drink.

5. What is the moral of this fable?

Ⓐ Haste makes waste.
Ⓑ Where there's a will, there's a way.
Ⓒ Look before you leap.
Ⓓ He who hesitates is lost.

Eight-year-old Tess heard her parents talking about her little brother Andrew. She realized something was wrong. Andrew was very sick, and they did not have enough money for his treatment. Tess heard her daddy say, "Only a miracle can save him now."

Tess went to her bedroom and retrieved a jar from its hiding place. There were a few coins in it. She counted them carefully. She then made her way to the drug store. The pharmacist was too busy to pay attention to her. "And what do you want?" he asked, annoyed at her persistence. "Can't you see that I am talking to my brother? He is here from Chicago."

Tess persisted, "My brother's really sick .... and I want to buy a miracle. His name is Andrew. He has something bad growing inside of his head and my daddy says only a miracle can save him now. So, how much does a miracle cost?" Tess rambled.

The pharmacist's brother, a well-dressed man, stooped down and asked the girl. "What kind of miracle does your brother need?"

"Don't know," replied Tess, eyes welling up with tears. "I just know Mommy says he needs an operation. But my daddy can't pay for it. So, I want to use my money."

The man from Chicago asked, "How much money do you have?"

"One dollar and eleven cents," said Tess.

"Well, what a coincidence," smiled the man.

"One dollar and eleven cents is the exact price of a miracle for your little brother." He took her money in one hand and grasped Tess's hand in the other. "Take me to where you live. I want to see your brother and meet your parents. Let's see if I have the kind of miracle you need."

The well-dressed man was Carlton Armstrong, a neurosurgeon. He operated on Andrew without charging any money. It wasn't long until Andrew was home and well again. "I wonder how much the surgery cost?" said Mother.

Tess smiled to herself. She knew exactly how much the miracle cost— one dollar and eleven cents.... plus the immense faith of a little child.

6. What is the message of this story?

- Ⓐ Parents care for their kids.
- Ⓑ Take good care of your health.
- Ⓒ Worrying solves problems.
- Ⓓ Miracles can happen when one has faith.

7. What is the moral of the above story?

- Ⓐ Tess was an eight-year-old girl.
- Ⓑ Sick people always get better by miracles.
- Ⓒ Miracles always happen.
- Ⓓ Persistence is more likely to get you what you want rather than doing nothing at all.

A GOOD PLAY

We built a ship upon the stairs,
All made of the back-bedroom chairs,
And filled it full of sofa pillows
To go a-sailing on the billows.
We took a saw and several nails,
And water in the nursery pails;
And Tom said, "Let us also take
An apple and a slice of cake";
—

Which was enough for Tom and me
To go a-sailing on, till tea.
We sailed along for days and days,
And had the very best of plays;
But Tom fell out and hurt his knee,
So there was no one left but me.

-By Robert Louis Stevenson
www.gutenburg.compublic domain

8. After reading this poem, what can you conclude about what happened? Circle the correct answer choice.

  Ⓐ Two boys were using their imagination while playing with make-believe ships on the stairs when one fell and was hurt.

  Ⓑ The poet likes to build ships everywhere.

  Ⓒ The boys played for days and days in the sea.

  Ⓓ Both B and C.

Challenge Yourself!

- **Applying Multiplication & Division**
- **Caring Characters & Life Lessons**

http://www.lumoslearning.com/a/dc3-3

Day 3

See Page 7 for Signup details

Day 4

1. Find the number that makes this equation true.
   n x 6 = 30

   Ⓐ n = 11
   Ⓑ n = 7
   Ⓒ n = 5
   Ⓓ n = 3

2. Find the number that makes this equation true.
   7 x ___ = 21

   Ⓐ 3
   Ⓑ 4
   Ⓒ 5
   Ⓓ 6

3. Find the number that makes this equation true.
   ___ x 4 = 36

   Ⓐ 9
   Ⓑ 8
   Ⓒ 7
   Ⓓ 6

4. Match the value of n for each of the equations given.

Equation	n=7	n=6
$3 \times 8 = 4 \times n$	○	○
$72 \div 9 = 56 \div n$	○	○

Day 4

Margaret was a simple lady who lived in a village with her husband, Robert. They had a daughter named Amy. Every day at sunrise, Margaret would wake up, cook, clean, and feed the cattle. Robert would milk the cows and then take the dogs for a long walk. Amy would study, help her mother for some time, and then get ready for school.

Amy studied in a school that was far away from her house, but she loved going to school. She went with her friends, Ingrid and Rebecca. They would walk together chatting, laughing, and singing songs as they went. They had to cross a river on the way. The only way they could cross it was by walking on a narrow bridge.

One day Margaret, Robert, Amy, and her friends were walking on the narrow bridge one behind the other. Amy and her friends were off to school as usual, Margaret and Robert wanted to go to the market on the other side of the river to buy groceries for the house.

As they were crossing the narrow bridge, Rebecca slipped. She gave a frightened scream, clutching Ingrid, who was in front of her. Both of them lost their balance and fell into the river. Amy clutched her mother in fright. For a moment, she hesitated, and then threw herself into the river after her friends, determined to save them.

Margaret screamed, and Robert jumped into the river. Some passers-by also jumped into the river and rescued the children, who were dripping wet, and shivering with fright.

That night, Robert patted his daughter Amy, and said, "You are a brave girl Amy, I'm proud of you."

5. Part A
In this story, Amy was scared but she jumped into the river. What caused Amy to ignore her fear?

Ⓐ Amy wanted to show off.
Ⓑ Amy wanted to escape.
Ⓒ Amy wanted to save her friends.
Ⓓ Amy wanted to join the fun.

Part B
Why did Robert jump into the river?

Ⓐ He wanted to save the girls.
Ⓑ He wanted to go for a swim.
Ⓒ He wanted to bathe in the river.
Ⓓ He was feeling hot.

One day, a baby elephant was happily dancing through the jungle, nodding his head and lifting up his trunk to trumpet loudly.

The loud sound woke up a monkey who was sleeping in a tree nearby. He was very angry. He scolded the elephant and asked him to keep quiet. "You silly animal," he said. "Can't you keep quiet? I'm sleeping."

"Oh, sorry," said the little elephant and walked on. After some time, the little elephant reached a river and saw some beautiful swans there. He gazed at the beautiful birds. The swans looked at him and began to laugh.

"Oh! Look at that big creature," they said. "What a long nose, his ears are like fans, and look at his skin, it's much too big for him. He looks like a big wrinkled bag with all of those folds!" They laughed at him, and swam away.

The little elephant was very sad. He tried to smooth out his skin with his trunk but it was no good. He thought, "Why am I so ugly? Let me hide so that no one can see me."

He tried to hide in a thick bush but he disturbed some nests. The birds flew above his head crying loudly while trying to at peck him.

The little elephant ran for cover. He went behind a big rock to hide. Suddenly, he saw a big bear coming towards him. It was growling and appeared to be very angry. The little elephant was very frightened and trumpeted loudly. Just as he trumpeted, he heard a loud crashing and stomping. A herd of elephants came charging to the rescue.

Seeing the herd of elephants, the frightened bear ran away.
The little elephant joyfully ran to the big elephants, thanked them, and said, "I wish I could be like you. You're so mighty and strong," he continued.

"But you are," replied the elephants. "You're a perfect little elephant." The little elephant danced for joy, he trumpeted loudly, and walked away happily with the other elephants following behind.

6. Which of the little elephant's actions showed it was happy?

- Ⓐ It danced along happily.
- Ⓑ It was walking thoughtfully.
- Ⓒ It was swaying from side to side.
- Ⓓ It was sleeping peacefully.

7. Why does the little elephant tell the other elephants, "I wish I could be like you"?

- Ⓐ He loved the elephants.
- Ⓑ He admired them because they were mighty and strong.
- Ⓒ He was not an elephant.
- Ⓓ He was frightened of them.

Maggie's Dilemma?

Maggie has many things to accomplish over the weekend. She wants to go to a friend's house for a party on Sunday afternoon. If she doesn't get her chores and homework done, she is afraid that her parents will not let her attend the party.

As she is getting ready for bed, Friday night, she is worrying and wondering how she can do everything before the party on Sunday. Her mother tells her that she needs to prioritize her life. Maggie is not sure what that means. She thinks to herself, "What is prioritize? How does that help me in my life?"

Her older brother, Ronny, comes into her room. He asks her, "Hey, Sis, why the puzzled look? Why are you just sitting there on your bed looking around your room?"

"Ronny, what does it mean when Mom tells me I need to prioritize my life?"
"What's wrong with my life?"

Ron laughs and tells her that she has a tendency to try to do too much stuff in too little time. He suggests that she make a list of what she needs to do. Then, she needs to make a list of what she WANTS to do. Again, Maggie looks confused.

He takes out one of her notebooks and starts to write. She watches as he puts his name at the top of the list along with the words - Have to Do. Then he makes numbers going down each side. He writes, clean room as number 1. For number 2, he puts down, take out the trash. Ron then writes down, mow the yard for number 3.

On another sheet of paper he does the same thing, only this time after his name he writes- Want to Do. On the second list the number 1 is watch wrestling on TV. Number 2 is play video games. Suddenly, Maggie gets it! "Oh, I see now. Prioritize means to put things in order of importance." Her brother replies, "Duh, I knew I could help out!" Ron laughs along with Maggie. She is no longer puzzled and starts to write.

8. What was the problem that Maggie was having? Select the correct answer by circling it.

Ⓐ She kept her room too messy.
Ⓑ She couldn't decide what her brother wanted her to do.
Ⓒ Maggie did not know how she could do everything she needed to do and wanted to do over the weekend.
Ⓓ None of the above.

Day 5

1. Which of these statements is not true?

Ⓐ 4 x (3 x 6) = (4 x 3) x 6
Ⓑ 4 x 3 = 3 x 4
Ⓒ 15 x 0 = 0 x 15
Ⓓ 12 x 1 = 12 x 12

2. Which of these statements is true?

Ⓐ The product of 11 x 6 is equal to the product of 6 x 11.
Ⓑ The product of 11 x 6 is greater than the product of 6 x 11.
Ⓒ The product of 11 x 6 is less than the product of 6 x 11.
Ⓓ There is no relationship between the product of 11 x 6 and the product of 6 x 11.

3. Which of the following expressions has a value of 0?

Ⓐ (3 x 4) x 1
Ⓑ 50 x 1
Ⓒ 3 x 4 x 0
Ⓓ (3 x 1) x 2

4. Match the property with the correct example.

	3 x (5 x 7) = (3 x 5) x 7	3 x 1 = 3	3 x 5 = 5 x 3	3 x (5 + 7) = (3 x 5) + (3 x 7)
Commutative Property	○	○	○	○
Associative Property	○	○	○	○
Identity Property	○	○	○	○
Distributive Property	○	○	○	○

One day, a baby elephant was happily dancing through the jungle, nodding his head and lifting up his trunk to trumpet loudly.

The loud sound woke up a monkey who was sleeping in a tree nearby. He was very angry. He scolded the elephant and asked him to keep quiet. "You silly animal," he said. "Can't you keep quiet? I'm sleeping."

"Oh, sorry," said the little elephant and walked on. After some time, the little elephant reached a river and saw some beautiful swans there. He gazed at the beautiful birds. The swans looked at him and began to laugh.

"Oh! Look at that big creature," they said. "What a long nose, his ears are like fans, and look at his skin, it's much too big for him. He looks like a big wrinkled bag with all of those folds!" They laughed at him, and swam away.

The little elephant was very sad. He tried to smooth out his skin with his trunk but it was no good. He thought, "Why am I so ugly? Let me hide so that no one can see me."

He tried to hide in a thick bush but he disturbed some nests. The birds flew above his head crying loudly while trying to at peck him.

The little elephant ran for cover. He went behind a big rock to hide. Suddenly, he saw a big bear coming towards him. It was growling and appeared to be very angry. The little elephant was very frightened and trumpeted loudly. Just as he trumpeted, he heard a loud crashing and stomping. A herd of elephants came charging to the rescue.

Seeing the herd of elephants, the frightened bear ran away.
The little elephant joyfully ran to the big elephants, thanked them, and said, "I wish I could be like you. You're so mighty and strong," he continued.

"But you are," replied the elephants. "You're a perfect little elephant." The little elephant danced for joy, he trumpeted loudly, and walked away happily with the other elephants following behind.

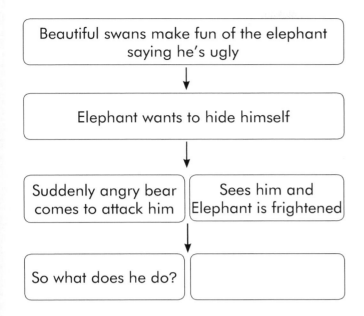

Beautiful swans make fun of the elephant saying he's ugly

↓

Elephant wants to hide himself

↓

Suddenly angry bear comes to attack him | Sees him and Elephant is frightened

↓

So what does he do?

5. Choose the correct set of words to fill in the blank.

- Ⓐ He asks the bear to leave him.
- Ⓑ He began to trumpet loudly.
- Ⓒ He ran as fast as he could.
- Ⓓ He was crying.

Margaret was a simple lady who lived in a village with her husband, Robert. They had a daughter named Amy. Every day at sunrise, Margaret would wake up, cook, clean, and feed the cattle. Robert would milk the cows and then take the dogs for a long walk. Amy would study, help her mother for some time, and then get ready for school.

Amy studied in a school that was far away from her house, but she loved going to school. She went with her friends, Ingrid and Rebecca. They would walk together chatting, laughing, and singing songs as they went. They had to cross a river on the way. The only way they could cross it was by walking on a narrow bridge.

One day Margaret, Robert, Amy, and her friends were walking on the narrow bridge one behind the other. Amy and her friends were off to school as usual, Margaret and Robert wanted to go to the market on the other side of the river to buy groceries for the house.

As they were crossing the narrow bridge, Rebecca slipped. She gave a frightened scream, clutching Ingrid, who was in front of her. Both of them lost their balance and fell into the river. Amy clutched her mother in fright. For a moment she hesitated and then threw herself into the river after her friends, determined to save them.

Margaret screamed, and Robert jumped into the river. Some passers-by also jumped into the river and rescued the children, who were dripping wet and shivering with fright.

That night Robert patted his daughter Amy and said, "You are a brave girl Amy, I'm proud of you."

6. What happened after Rebecca grabbed Ingrid on the bridge?

Ⓐ Margaret and Robert went on the other side of the river.
Ⓑ Robert screamed.
Ⓒ The girls fell into the river.
Ⓓ Margaret helped her family by cooking and cleaning.

1) I was very mad at my sister for eating the cookie.
(2) "Why did you eat the last cookie?" I asked.
(3) Sister ate the last cookie in the cookie jar.
(4) "Sorry," she said, "I was really hungry."

7. Which of the following answers best shows the chain of events?

Ⓐ 3,1,4,2
Ⓑ 3,1,2,4
Ⓒ 1,2,3,4
Ⓓ 2,3,4,1

Playing Video Games

Scotty loves to play video games! I mean he plays every chance he gets. He even plays when he should be doing his homework, chores or going to bed! It has gotten so bad that his parents are considering a punishment to teach him a lesson.

Scotty doesn't understand why they are upset with him and is trying to figure out what he can do so that he doesn't get his video game machine taken away. He has asked his friends for their ideas on the subject, too. He even asked his counselor at school. Scotty has been seeing her since his grades started dropping. The counselor told him it is very simple, give up the game playing on his own and get back to doing homework, chores, and going to bed on time.

To Scotty, the ideas his counselor told him are good, but he is very reluctant to do it. So one of his friends, Hailey, has offered to help. She is going to make him a chart of time spent on playing games compared to time spent on his responsibilities. He agrees to give it a try.

The following is his chart for the first week.

	Monday	Tuesday	Wednesday	Thursday	Friday	Saturday	Sunday	Totals
Playing Video Games	4 hours	4 hours	3 hours	3 hours	2 hours	3 hours	3 hours	22 hours
Doing Home-work	30 min	30 min	1 hour	1 hour	1 hour	none	none	4 hours
Doing Chores	15 min	15 min	45 min	45 min	45 min	2 hours	1 hour	5 hours 45 min
Going to Bed On Time	Not done	Not done	Not done	Done	Not done	Done	Done	Went to be on time 3 days

8. **Has Scotty's attitude toward doing his homework and chores improved or not? Select the correct answer choice and write it in the box given below.**

   Ⓐ His attitude has not improved during the first week.
   Ⓑ His attitude has shown some improvement.
   Ⓒ There is no change in his behavior.

Challenge Yourself!

- **Multiplication and Division Properties**
- **A Chain of Events**

http://www.lumoslearning.com/a/dc3-5

Day 5

See Page 7 for Signup details

Learn Sign Language

What is American Sign Language?

American Sign Language (ASL) is a complete, complex language that employs signs made by moving the hands combined with facial expressions and postures of the body. It is the primary language of many North Americans who are deaf and is one of several communication options used by people who are deaf or hard-of-hearing.

Where did ASL originate?

The exact beginnings of ASL are not clear, but some suggest that it arose more than 200 years ago from the intermixing of local sign languages and French Sign Language (LSF, or Langue des Signes Française). Today's ASL includes some elements of LSF plus the original local sign languages, which over the years have melded and changed into a rich, complex, and mature language. Modern ASL and modern LSF are distinct languages and, while they still contain some similar signs, can no longer be understood by each other's users.

Source: https://www.nidcd.nih.gov/health/american-sign-language

Why should one learn sign language?

Enrich your cognitive skills: Sign language can enrich the cognitive development of a child. Since, different cognitive skills can be acquired as a child, learning sign language, can be implemented with practice and training in early childhood.

Make new friends: You could communicate better with the hearing-impaired people you meet, if you know the sign language, it is easier to understand and communicate effectively.

Volunteer: Use your ASL skills to interpret as a volunteer. volunteers can help in making a real difference in people's lives, with their time, effort and commitment.

Bilingual: If you are monolingual, here is an opportunity to become bilingual, with a cause.

Private chat: It would be useful to converse with a friend or in a group without anyone understanding, what you are up to.

Let's Learn the Alphabets

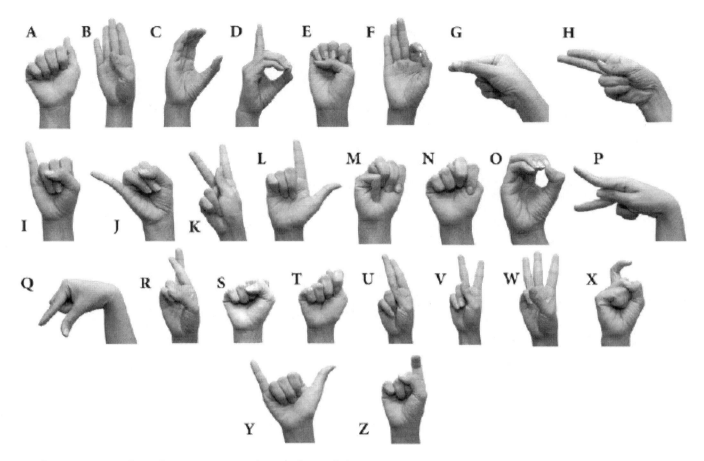

Sign language is fun if it is practiced with friends!
Partner with your friends or family members and try the following activities.

Activity

1. Communicate the following to your friend using the ASL.
   - USA
   - ASL

If your friend hasn't mastered the ASL yet, give the above alphabet chart to your friend.

2. Try saying your name in ASL using the hand gestures.

3. Have your friend communicate a funny word using ASL and you try to read it without the help of the chart. List the words you tried below.

Let's Learn the Numbers

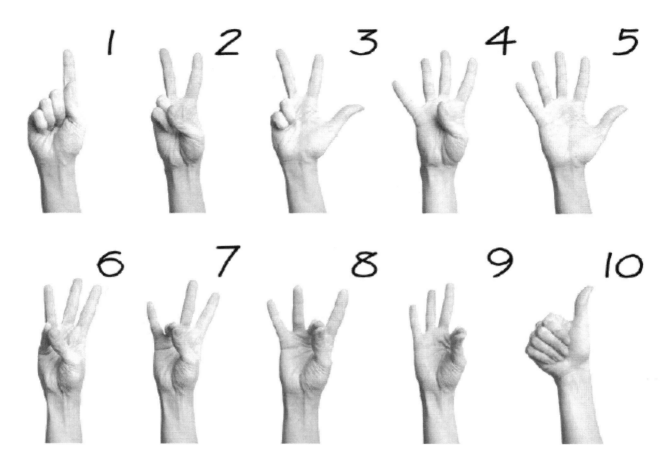

Activity:

1. Share your postal code through ASL to your friend.
2. Communicate your home phone number in ASL to your friend.

Let's Learn Some Words

RED

ORANGE

YELLOW

GREEN

PURPLE

BLUE

EAT

DRINK

MORE

PLEASE

THANK YOU

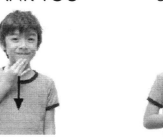

SORRY

This Week's Online Activities

- **Reading Assignment**
- **Vocabulary Practice**
- **Write Your Summer Diary**

https://www.lumoslearning.com/a/slh3-4

See Page 7 for Signup details

Weekly Fun Summer Photo Contest

Take a picture of your summer fun activity and share it on Twitter or Instagram

Use the **#SummerLearning** mention

@LumosLearning on Twitter or

@lumos.learning on Instagram

Tag friends and increase your chances of winning the contest

Participate and stand a chance to WIN $50 Amazon gift card!

Week 2 Summer Practice

Relating Multiplication & Division (3.OA.B.6)

1. Find the number that would complete both of the following number sentences.

    ___ x 6 = 30
    30 ÷ 6 = ___

    (A) 7
    (B) 5
    (C) 6
    (D) 24

2. Find the number that would complete both of the following number sentences.

    7 x ___ = 21
    21 ÷ ___ = 7

    (A) 5
    (B) 14
    (C) 3
    (D) 7

3. Find the number that would complete both of the following number sentences.

    72 ÷ ___ = 8
    8 x ___ = 72

    (A) 8
    (B) 9
    (C) 10
    (D) 64

4. Part A
For the expression below, Circle the correct symbol to be filled in the blank.

40 ÷ 5 ____ 54 ÷ 9

Ⓐ =
Ⓑ >
Ⓒ <

Part B
For the expression below, Circle the correct symbol to be filled in the blank.

35 ÷ 7 ____ 28 ÷ 4

Ⓐ =
Ⓑ >
Ⓒ <

Part C
For the expression below, Circle the correct symbol to be filled in the blank.

18 ÷ 6 ____ 24 ÷ 8

Ⓐ =
Ⓑ >
Ⓒ <

Figurative Language Expressions (RL.3.4)

Day 1

5. What is the meaning of the phrase "can't go on"?

Ⓐ Cannot go back
Ⓑ Cannot switch it on
Ⓒ Cannot continue
Ⓓ Cannot stop fighting

6. What does the underlined phrase mean in this stanza?

I quarreled with my brother
I don't know what about,
One thing led to another
And somehow <u>we fell out</u>.
The start of it was slight,
The end of it was strong,
He said he was right,
I knew he was wrong!
~Eleanor Farjeon

- Ⓐ had a disagreement
- Ⓑ fell down
- Ⓒ fainted
- Ⓓ were pushed out

7. What is the meaning of the word "charging up" in the following sentence?

Just as he trumpeted, he heard a loud crashing and stamping. A herd of wrinkled elephants came <u>charging up</u>.

- Ⓐ walked away
- Ⓑ walked slowly forward
- Ⓒ came up to dance
- Ⓓ rushed forward to attack

NASA facts and terms

NASA, National Aeronautics and Space Administration began in 1958. This occurred one year after the Soviets launched Sputnik 1. Sputnik 1 was the first artificial satellite in the entire world. This began what was known as the "space race" between Russia and the United States. NASA has excelled in many areas in space science. The greatest is that of having manned (human) space missions.

Here is a list of those:
U.S. Manned Space Programs

- Mercury: the first U.S. program for human spaceflight
- Gemini: the first two-man crews, longer missions
- Apollo: the first spaceflights to the moon
- Skylab: a place where humans lived and worked in space for extended periods of time
- Apollo-Soyuz: first international manned spaceflight
- Space shuttle: the first reusable spacecraft
- International Space Station: an effort to create a permanent orbiting laboratory in space

The following vocabulary helps you to better understand when reading about NASA and its accomplishments. Study the vocabulary, match the vocabulary to definitions. Then fill in the blanks using the context sentences.

Aeronautics - Science dealing with the operation of aircraft.

Astronaut - A person who pilots a spacecraft or works in space; a space traveler, particularly one from the United States. For example, Alan B Shepard Jr was the commander of a number of NASA space missions.

Johnson Space Center - The headquarters for all U.S. manned spacecraft projects conducted by NASA; the location of the Mission Control Center for manned space flights.

Kennedy Space Center - The launch facility for all U.S. space missions that carry crews.

Launch vehicle - A powerful rocket used to launch a spacecraft or satellite into space.

NASA (National Aeronautics & Space Administration) - The government agency whose mission is to research and develop safe and meaningful ways to explore space.

Orbit - The path of a spacecraft or a heavenly body as it revolves around a planet or other body.

Space shuttle - A reusable space vehicle that takes off like a rocket and lands like an airplane.

Space station - An orbiting spacecraft designed to be occupied by teams of astronauts or cosmonauts over a long period.

8. Match the vocabulary with the definition. Write the correct definition against each of the words given.

> A. headquarters of US manned spacecraft projects and location of Mission Control
> B. the science of space craft operation
> C. government agency in charge of space exploration
> D. launch facility in Cape Canaveral, FL
> E. orbiting space craft designed for occupancy for long period of time
> F. a reusable space craft, takes off like a rocket, lands like a plane
> G. powerful rocket used to launch space craft or satellite
> H. a person who operates spacecraft or works in space, from US
> I. path of a spacecraft or heavenly body as it goes around a planet

Definition	Vocabulary
NASA	C. government agency in charge of space exploration
Launch vehicle	
Aeronautics	
Astronaut	
Space shuttle	
Orbit	
Johnson Space Center	
Kennedy Space Center	
Space Station	

Challenge Yourself!

- Relating Multiplication & Division
- Figurative Language Expressions

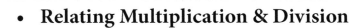

http://www.lumoslearning.com/a/dc3-6

Day 1

See Page 7 for Signup details

Day 2

1. Find the product.

6 x 0 = ____

- Ⓐ 6
- Ⓑ 1
- Ⓒ 0
- Ⓓ 2

2. Find the product.

1 x 10 = ____

- Ⓐ 0
- Ⓑ 1
- Ⓒ 10
- Ⓓ 11

3. Solve.

3 x 8 = ____

- Ⓐ 24
- Ⓑ 21
- Ⓒ 18
- Ⓓ 28

4. Complete the following table.

5	x	8	=	
8	÷		=	8
	÷	7	=	0
6	x		=	30

Camels are bumpy,
Their backs are all lumpy,
Giraffes are long- legged and meek:
Bears are so growly,
Hyenas are howly,
Dolphins are slippery and sleek.

Kangaroos have a pocket,
But no way to lock it,
Their babies can look out and peep,
But monkeys are funny
I wish I had money,
Enough to buy one and keep.

5. The above poem has two _____ .

    Ⓐ stanzas
    Ⓑ paragraphs
    Ⓒ passages
    Ⓓ parts

An astronomer used to go out every night to observe stars. Often, he would be seen with a telescope in one hand and a notebook in the other. One evening, while he wandered through the suburbs with his attention fixed on the sky, he accidentally fell into a deep uncovered well. He cried out loudly for help. As he waited to be rescued, he moaned and howled about his sores and bruises. His neighbor was passing by and happened to hear his wailing and weeping. He quickly helped him out of the well. After he came to know how the accident happened, this is what he said to the astronomer: "Hark you old fellow, why in striving to pry into heaven, do you not manage to see what is on earth?"

6. What line from the paragraph tells the reader where the astronomer lived?

    Ⓐ One evening, while he wandered through the suburbs.
    Ⓑ He quickly helped him out of the well.
    Ⓒ He would often be seen with a telescope in one hand and a notebook in the other.
    Ⓓ It does not tell us where he lived.

PART II. THE FIREBRAND IN THE FOREST

When the two women saw that the wolf had the firebrand, they were very angry, and straightway they ran after him.

"Catch it and run!" cried the wolf, and he threw it to the deer. The deer caught it and ran.
"Catch it and run!" cried the deer, and he threw it to the bear. The bear caught it and ran.
"Catch it and fly!" cried the bear, and he threw it to the bat. The bat caught it and flew.
"Catch it and run!" cried the bat, and he threw it to the squirrel. The squirrel caught it and ran.

"Oh, serpent," called the two old women, "you are no friend to the First Americans. Help us. Get the firebrand away from the squirrel."

As the squirrel ran swiftly over the ground, the serpent sprang up and tried to seize the firebrand. He did not get it, but the smoke went into the squirrel's nostrils and made him cough. He would not let go of the firebrand, but ran and ran till he could throw it to the frog.

When the frog was running away with it, the squirrel for the first time thought of himself, and he found that his beautiful bushy tail was no longer straight, for the fire had curled it up over his back.

"Do not be sorry," called the young First American across the pond. "Whenever a First American boy sees a squirrel with his tail curled up over his back, he will throw him a nut."

PART III. THE FIREBRAND IN THE POND

All this time the firebrand was burning, and the frog was going to the pond as fast as he could. The old women were running after him, and when he came to the water, one of them caught him by the tail.

"I have caught him!" she called.
"Do not let him go!" cried the other.

"No, I will not," said the first; but she did let him go, for the little frog tore himself away and dived into the water. His tail was still in the woman's hand, but the firebrand was safe, and he made his way swiftly across the pond.

Here it is," said the frog.

"Where?" asked the young First American. Then the frog coughed, and out of his mouth came the firebrand. It was small, for it had been burning all this time, but it set fire to the leaves and twigs, and soon the First Americans were warm again. They sang and they danced about the flames.

This is from the work How Fire Was Brought to the First Americans by Cyrus MacMillian.

7. What are the bold parts of this selection called?

Ⓐ titles
Ⓑ parts
Ⓒ headings
Ⓓ topics

"A Little Road Not Made Of Man"
By Emily Elizabeth Dickinson

A little road not made of man,
Enabled of the eye,
Accessible to thill of bee,
Or cart of butterfly.

If town it have, beyond itself,
'T is that I cannot say;
I only sigh, -- no vehicle
Bears me along that way.

8. Which are the correct rhyming words in patterns from the poem? Circle the correct answer choice.

Ⓐ man, can, eye, bee.
Ⓑ eye, butterfly, say, way.
Ⓒ butterfly, sigh, eye, way.
Ⓓ road, cart, eye, butterfly.

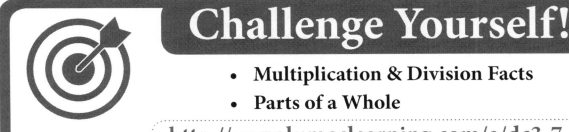

Day 3

1. Danny has 47 baseball cards. He gives his brother 11 cards. Danny then divides the remaining cards between 3 of his classmates. How many cards does each classmate receive?

   Ⓐ 15
   Ⓑ 3
   Ⓒ 12
   Ⓓ 11

2. Two third grade classes are lined up outside. One class is lined up in 3 rows of 7. The other class is lined up in 4 rows of 5. How many total third graders are lined up outside?

   Ⓐ 19 third graders
   Ⓑ 21 third graders
   Ⓒ 41 third graders
   Ⓓ 20 third graders

3. Jessica earns 10 dollars per hour for babysitting. She has saved 60 dollars so far. How many more hours will she need to babysit to buy something that costs 100 dollars?

   Ⓐ 40 hours
   Ⓑ 6 hours
   Ⓒ 10 hours
   Ⓓ 4 hours

4. A farmer collected 22 pints of milk from his cows. He put all the milk into bottles. Each bottle holds 2 pints of milk. He accidentally spilled 6 bottles of milk. How many bottles are left with the farmer now? Circle the math sentences that can be used to find the answer. (Circle all correct answers)

   Ⓐ 11
   Ⓑ 24
   Ⓒ 16
   Ⓓ 5

I had a silver buckle,
I sewed it on my shoe,
And 'neath a sprig of mistletoe
I danced the evening through!
I had a bunch of cowslips,
I hid 'em in a grot,
In case the elves should come by night
And me remember not.
I had a yellow ribbon,
I tied it in my hair,
That, walking in the garden,
The birds might see it there.
I had a secret laughter,
I laughed it near the wall:
Only the ivy and the wind
May tell of it at all.

By Walter de la Mare (1873-1956), under the pseudonym Walter Ramal, title unknown, from Songs of Childhood, published 1902.

5. Who is the narrator of this poem?

Ⓐ the birds
Ⓑ an elf
Ⓒ I (the writer, author)
Ⓓ the ivy

Pearl reached in her pocket for the coins, but she could not feel them. Desperately, she pulled everything out of her pocket. She found a chocolate wrapper, a bus pass, her student ID card, lipstick, mascara, and her cell phone. There were NO coins!

6. Who is telling this story about Pearl?

Ⓐ Pearl
Ⓑ Pearl's mother
Ⓒ a narrator
Ⓓ the bus driver

The Goose that Laid the Golden Egg

A man once had a goose I'm told,
Which had laid each day an egg of gold.
Now if this treasure were well spent,
It might make any one content.
But no! This man desired more;
And though of eggs he had rich store;
He thought one day the goose he'd kill,

And then at once his pockets fill.
So chasing goosey round and round,
She soon was caught and firmly bound
He opened her from neck to tail
And then his folly did bewail.
For not a single egg was there,
And thus he lost this treasure rare.

7. Who is telling the story in this poem? Mark "Yes" or "No" against each character.

	Yes	No
The man	○	○
The goose	○	○
A narrator, outside of the story	○	○
The golden eggs	○	○

School Rules

The students at Morgan Lane Elementary are very upset with some of the new rules. Starting this year, they can no longer have rolling carts to carry their books, lunches, and personal items. The school board became concerned about what some kids might be hiding in the backpacks and rolling carts. Also, last spring, one of the students was hurt when another student's cart hit them in the hallway. Parents are a little upset, but they understand that for safety and security of the students and staff, this is a good idea. The new rule states that only clear see-through backpacks will be allowed. Even students' lunches have to be able to be seen.

This is not making the students happy at all. Mrs. Logan's third graders have been talking about it all morning. Most of them had already bought their carts and colored backpacks before the rule was adopted by the school board. So here on the first day of school, they are lugging around everything. The stores ran out of the clear see-through backpacks quickly. Some parents just couldn't afford to purchase additional items at such a late date when they had already bought others before.

Needless to say all of this chatter in class, has made it rough on Mrs. Logan to teach on the first day.

She has decided to stop her lesson and have a class discussion. She is using a chart to show good reasons for the changes and to show students concerns about the changes. It also shows possible alternatives or solutions for problems that are being brought up by the students.

Here is what the chart looks like so far.

Positive Effects of New Rule	Negative Effects of New Rule	Possible Alternatives or Solutions
Fewer accidents with carts	Students who are small in size cannot carry backpacks without injury to their backs.	Put in lockers for students so they do not have to worry about carrying so much that is visible to all.
No worries about things that are unrelated to school being in backpacks	Handicap students unable to get around with backpacks	Hold an awareness session to fully explain situations behind the decision
Students and staff are better protected.	Feeling of unrest and not trusting students.	Allow small non-see through bags for personal items.

8. Give two reasons why you feel the rule is good, 2 more reasons why it is a problem and 2 more solutions. Write your answer in the box below.

Challenge Yourself!

- **Two-Step Problems**
- **Who's Talking Now?**

http://www.lumoslearning.com/a/dc3-8

Day 3

See Page 7 for Signup details

Day 4

1. Which of the following is an even number?

Ⓐ 764,723
Ⓑ 90,835
Ⓒ 5,862
Ⓓ 609

2. Which of these sets contains no odd numbers?

Ⓐ 13, 15, 81, 109, 199
Ⓑ 123, 133, 421, 412, 600
Ⓒ 34, 46, 48, 106, 88
Ⓓ 12, 37, 6, 14, 144

3. Complete the following statement.
   The sum of two even numbers will always be _____ .

Ⓐ greater than 10
Ⓑ less than 100
Ⓒ even
Ⓓ odd

4. For each statement in the first column, choose all the correct answers.

	2	4	5	7
A number has a four in its ones place. The number can be a multiple of _____.	○	○	○	○
A number has a five in its ones place. The number can be a multiple of _____.	○	○	○	○
A number has a zero in its ones place. The number can be a multiple of _____.	○	○	○	○
A number has a three in its ones place. The number can be a multiple of _____.	○	○	○	○

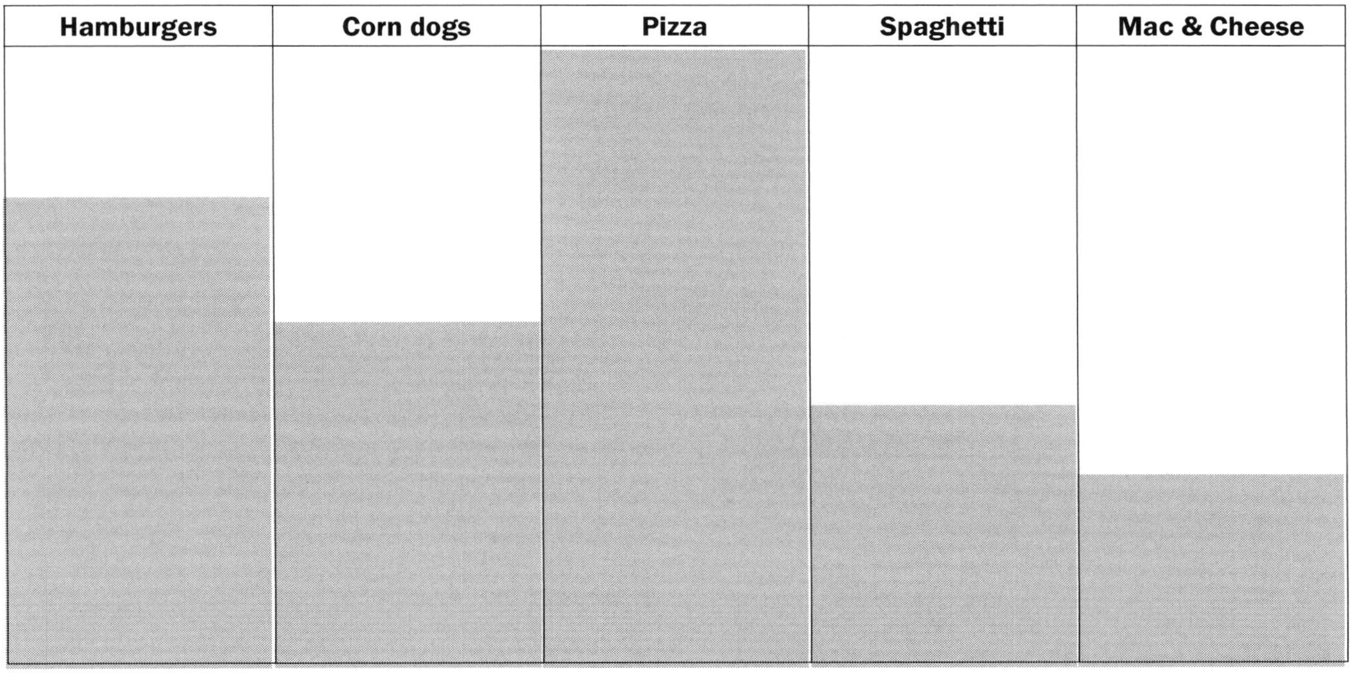

Hamburgers	Corn dogs	Pizza	Spaghetti	Mac & Cheese

Look at the graph above and answer the following questions about the lunch menu at Curbside School.

5. What is the most popular item on the lunch menu?

Ⓐ Hamburgers
Ⓑ Corn dogs
Ⓒ Pizza
Ⓓ Spaghetti
Ⓔ Mac & cheese

6. What addition to the graph would make it easier for you to decide which item is liked almost as much as spaghetti?

Ⓐ Pictures
Ⓑ Headings
Ⓒ Food descriptions
Ⓓ Numbers

7. Which item is the students' second favorite?

Ⓐ Hamburgers
Ⓑ Corn dogs
Ⓒ Pizza
Ⓓ Spaghetti
Ⓔ Mac & cheese

Playing Video Games

Scotty loves to play video games! I mean he plays every chance he gets. He even plays when he should be doing his homework, chores or going to bed! It has gotten so bad that his parents are considering a punishment to teach him a lesson.

Scotty doesn't understand why they are upset with him and is trying to figure out what he can do so that he doesn't get his video game machine taken away. He has asked his friends for their ideas on the subject, too. He even asked his counselor at school. Scotty has been seeing her since his grades started dropping. The counselor told him it is very simple, give up the game playing on his own and get back to doing homework, chores, and going to bed on time.

To Scotty, the ideas his counselor told him are good, but he is very reluctant to do it. So one of his friends, Hailey, has offered to help. She is going to make him a chart of time spent on playing games compared to time spent on his responsibilities. He agrees to give it a try.

8. Based on this chart, complete the chart totals. For "Going to Bed On Time", count the days he did go to bed on time.

	Monday	Tuesday	Wednesday	Thursday	Friday	Saturday	Sunday	Totals
Playing Video Games	4 hours	4 hours	3 hours	3 hours	2 hours	3 hours	3 hours	
Doing Homework	30 min	30 min	1 hour	1 hour	1 hour	none	none	
Doing Chores	15 min	15 min	45 min	45 min	45 min	2 hours	1 hour	
Going to Bed On Time	Not done	Not done	Not done	Done	Not done	Done	Done	

Day 5

1. What is the value of the 9 in 11,291?

Ⓐ 9 ones
Ⓑ 9 hundreds
Ⓒ 9 thousands
Ⓓ 9 tens

2. What is the value of the digit 6 in 36,801?

Ⓐ Six thousand
Ⓑ Sixty
Ⓒ Sixty thousand
Ⓓ Six hundred

3. Which of these numbers has a 9 in the thousands place?

Ⓐ 690,099
Ⓑ 900
Ⓒ 209,866
Ⓓ 90,786

4. Complete the table in the format given in the example.

Number	Number when rounded to the nearest ten	Number when rounded to the nearest hundred
2,349	2,350	2,300
4,092		
8,396		

Day 5

One day, a baby elephant was happily dancing through the jungle, nodding his head and lifting up his trunk to trumpet loudly.

The loud sound woke up a monkey who was sleeping in a tree nearby. He was very angry. He scolded the elephant and asked him to keep quiet.

"You silly animal," he said. "Can't you keep quiet? I'm sleeping."

"Oh, sorry," said the little elephant and walked on. After some time, the little elephant reached a river and saw some beautiful swans there. He gazed at the beautiful birds. The swans looked at him and began to laugh.

"Oh! Look at that big creature," they said. "What a long nose, his ears are like fans, and look at his skin, it's much too big for him. He looks like a big wrinkled bag with all those folds!" They laughed at him and swam away.

The little elephant was very sad. He tried to smooth out his skin with his trunk but it was no good. He thought, "Why am I so ugly? Let me hide so that no one can see me."

He tried to hide in a thick bush but he disturbed some nests. The birds flew above his head crying loudly and tried to peck him.

The little elephant ran for cover. He went behind a big rock to hide. Suddenly, he saw a big bear coming towards him. It was growling and appeared to be very angry. The little elephant was very frightened and trumpeted loudly. Just as he trumpeted, he heard a loud crashing and stomping. A herd of elephants came charging to the rescue.

Seeing the herd the frightened bear ran away.

The little elephant joyfully ran to the big elephants, thanked them, and said, "I wish I could be like you. You're so mighty and strong," he continued.

"But you are," replied the elephants. "You're a perfect little elephant." The little elephant danced for joy, he trumpeted loudly, and walked away happily with the other elephants following behind.

5. What was different about the little elephant from the other animals?

Ⓐ He is smaller than the other animals.
Ⓑ He looks different than the other animals.
Ⓒ He is weaker than the other animals.
Ⓓ He is quieter than the other animals.

6. Who is the little elephant most like in this story?

Ⓐ The other elephants
Ⓑ The bear
Ⓒ The birds
Ⓓ The monkey

An astronomer used to go out every night to observe stars. Often, he would be seen with a telescope in one hand and a notebook in the other. One evening, while he wandered through the suburbs with his attention fixed on the sky, he accidentally fell into a deep uncovered well. He cried out loudly for help. As he waited to be rescued, he moaned and howled about his sores and bruises. His neighbor was passing by and happened to hear his wailing and weeping. He quickly helped him out of the well. After he came to know how the accident happened, this is what he said to the astronomer: "Hark you old fellow, why in striving to pry into heaven, do you not manage to see what is on earth?"

7. How is the neighbor different than the astronomer?

Ⓐ The neighbor is more interested in the sky than the astronomer is.
Ⓑ The astronomer is awake at night while the neighbor is asleep.
Ⓒ The astronomer likes to read, but the neighbor does not.
Ⓓ The neighbor is concerned with things on earth while the astronomer is concerned with things in the sky.

The New Year Celebrations in Different Countries

In the United States, the New Year begins every January 1st. On the night before, most people celebrate the coming of the New Year right before and when the clock strikes 12:00am. People generally make what is called "New Year's Resolutions". In doing so, they choose something that they want to change or make better in their lives. Some may decide to lose weight, to save money, to get along better with others, or even to quit a bad habit. The resolution is supposed to be kept and followed

all during the year. It is a kind of promise a person makes to themselves. People tend to break self-made promises early on in the year.

Chinese New Year

The Chinese New Year, commonly called the Spring Festival in China is celebrated at the changing of the traditional lunisolar calendar"-Chinese calendar. The Chinese celebrate beginning on the first new moon, between what we in the United States know as January 21 and February 20. The Chinese start their celebrations on the evening before and continue to celebrate through until around the 15th day of their first calendar month. The Chinese New Year is centuries old and began as a time to honor ancestors and people of high ranking political and religious statuses. Many of the customs of Chinese New Year continue to be followed not only in China, other Chinese influenced countries, but in the United States, as well. These include the annual family dinner, the complete house cleaning to ward off evil and welcome good, and the many parades, brightly decorated costumes, and wall hangings.

The Indian New Year

Ugadi is the official name given to the festival celebrated as the New Year in India. The name, Ugadi, means the beginning of a new age. It is celebrated on the first day of the Hindu month, Chaitra, thus marking the beginning of spring. It is thought that the Lord Brahma began creation on this day according to Hindu culture. The celebration is highlighted by the serving of magnificent meals. The festival is also known for the cleaning of houses, and wearing of new clothes. In the India calendar, each year has a name. There are 60 names and the names are repeated every 60 years.

8. What ways are the celebrations in the China and India similar to one another? Circle the correct answer choice

    Ⓐ The celebrations occur at different times and have no similarities.
    Ⓑ In both China and India, houses are cleaned and expansive meals are served.
    Ⓒ The calendars seem to be similar to one another.
    Ⓓ None of the above.

Challenge Yourself!

- **Rounding Numbers**
- **Alike and Different**

http://www.lumoslearning.com/a/dc3-10

See Page 7 for Signup details

Day 5

7 Simple Ways To Improve Your Road Skating

There is no better feeling than the freedom you feel from Road Skating. It is unlike anything else. The wind through your hair as you glide down the road on a beautiful sunny day. The breeze keeping you cool while you enjoy yourself. It is truly a magical feeling. Like anything else in life, you want to have fun while improving, you are careful when playing. Here are seven simple ways to improve on your road skating.

1. Choosing the perfect skates for you

Before you can get out there and start skating, you need to decide what type of skates you want to wear. There are two different types of skates you can choose from. The first type of skates are called inline skates. These have four wheels together in a straight line, going down the middle, from the front to the back of the skate. They look similar to ice skates, but are for using outdoors or on a hardwood surface. Inline skates are the more common of the two yet are a little harder to learn to use.

The second type of skates are called quad skates. Quads have two wheels in the front and two wheels in the back. Most quads will have a stopper in the front by the toe. This allows skaters to stop quicker and easier. Inline skates usually don't have a stopper, but there are some that do have one at the back of the skate.

Both skates have their strengths and weaknesses. Each type of skate has a unique feel to the way you skate in them. Some people don't like inlines because of the lack of feeling safe, others believe they are safer than skating with quads. You should try the two styles out and see what feels more natural for you.

2. Dress appropriately

It is important to dress appropriately. It seems like something you automatically do, but it is just as important as anything else. If it's a cool breezy day you might want to wear windbreaker pants and a t-shirt. On hot days, shorts would be a better dress option. Wearing a hat or sunglasses is useful in keeping the sun out of your eyes. Preparing an outfit for the day will help keep you cool outside.

3. Check the weather for the day

Weather will be a factor in deciding when to go out. It doesn't just factor in to how you dress. It also will determine if that day is good to skate at all. A beautiful day will bring hours of fun, but bad weather is never good. If there is inclimate weather in the forecast than it may be a good idea to hold off on skating. Don't get caught in the rain because you forgot to check.

4. Safety first when skating

Safely skating is a good way to make sure that you can have a great time without any serious injuries. You should never go out without proper safety equipment. When getting ready, check and make sure you have everything you need. First thing you will need is a helmet. Helmets are a cool way to express yourself and keep your head safe. Helmets come in a variety of styles and colors, and can be a way to show your unique personality to everyone else around you.

Elbow pads and knee pads are also necessary when getting ready. When we are Road Skating we will fall from time to time. It happens to everyone and is just part of skating. Elbow pads and knee pads will help keep you unharmed whenever this happens. They keep us from getting scraped up, which doesn't feel so good. Wrist guards should be worn as well. Naturally, when we fall, we put our hands down to stop us. Wrist guards help protect your wrists from getting damaged when this happens.

5. Practice makes perfect: don't be scared to fail

Like anything in life, the more you practice something the easier it will come to you. It takes time and effort to become better at anything you do. We evolve everyday as we continue to strive to get better. Failing is something we have to deal with whenever working towards our goals. If everything in life came easily then there would be no competitive spirit.The drive to be better makes things in life worth working towards. It is good to be scared sometimes. Fear brings out the best in you, but don't let it overwhelm you. If you fall, get back up and try again. At the moment it may seem pointless to continue, but the outcome will be rewarding.

6. Don't skate on an empty stomach and keep hydrated

Skating takes a lot of energy. Eating a good meal is very important when planning a day of roller exercise. Give yourself at least a half hour to digest your food before going out. Water is key too. Staying hydrated will keep you going throughout the day. It is important to have plenty of water ready as needed. Water and a good meal are essential.

7. Have fun while skating

Skating is meant to be fun. You should be able to be yourself and not worry about being judged by others. Just remember, if it wasn't fun than you probably wouldn't want to be doing it. Having fun while skating will make all that practice seem Lee's like practice and more like an activity.
Following these simple guidelines will help you become a better skater. You will get better the more you practice, and having fun while doing it will make you want to practice more often. Everything will fall into place if you let it. Remember, we earn everything we get so how you go about getting there will determine the success you have in your attempts.

This Week's Online Activities

- Reading Assignment
- Vocabulary Practice
- Write Your Summer Diary

https://www.lumoslearning.com/a/slh3-4

See Page 7 for Signup details

Weekly Fun Summer Photo Contest

Take a picture of your summer fun activity and share it on Twitter or Instagram

Use the **#SummerLearning** mention

@LumosLearning on Twitter or

@lumos.learning on Instagram

Tag friends and increase your chances of winning the contest

Participate and stand a chance to WIN $50 Amazon gift card!

Day 1

1. What is the standard form of 70,000 + 6,000 + 800 + 60 + 2?

Ⓐ 706,862
Ⓑ 76,862
Ⓒ 7,682
Ⓓ 782

2. Two numbers have a difference of 29. The two numbers could be _____.

Ⓐ 11 and 18
Ⓑ 23 and 42
Ⓒ 40 and 11
Ⓓ 50 and 39

3. Two numbers add up to 756. One number is 356. What is the other number?

Ⓐ 356
Ⓑ 300
Ⓒ 400
Ⓓ 456

4. Type in the correct numbers to make the sum true.

	Hundreds	Tens	Ones
	2		5
+		3	
Total	8	4	9

Brandon lived with his mother at one end of the forest. His school was at the other end of the forest. Every day he had to go through the forest to get to school and the forest was very scary.

One day he told his mother that he felt very scared to cross that forest.

His mother said, "Don't be scared" "Your brother lives in the forest. Whenever you get scared, you can always call him. He won't answer you but he will see that no harm comes to you."

Brandon said, "Why did you not tell me about my brother earlier? What is his name?"

Mother said, "His name is Courage. Whenever you get frightened, call his name, and he will silently follow you to school and see that you come back home safely."

The next day Brandon was happy to get ready for school. He was not scared as he went through the forest on the way to school. That day, while coming home from school, he got scared when he heard the sounds of animals. He then remembered his mother's words that his brother would protect him whenever he was frightened.

Brandon called out "Courage, Courage" with full confidence. Suddenly he began to feel better. He began to feel brave. He again called out, "Courage!, Courage!" He thought that his brother was silently following him, he began to sing softly and then loudly. He realized that he was not frightened after all. He crossed the forest confidently with courage.

The only thing we need to have is confidence and courage in ourselves to move ahead.

5. Where did Brandon live?

6. In what setting does Brandon find his courage?

Ⓐ the forest
Ⓑ his house
Ⓒ school
Ⓓ his friend's house

7. Which is a likely setting for this story?

Ⓐ a jungle
Ⓑ a zoo
Ⓒ a forest
Ⓓ on an African safari

Jasmine nervously left the car. She and her parents had been riding for what seemed like days, but after ten hours, they were finally here. She carefully studied the old farmhouse. "Are you ready?" her dad asked. Jasmine only shrugged. She had talked with her "G", as the kind lady had referred to herself, a few times on the phone, but at the age of eight, she had never actually met her grandma. It seemed that work, school, or illness had kept her away.

Jasmine's parents had told her stories about her "G" and that she had met her when she was only a few months old, but in Jasmine's mind this was the first time. She exited the car and was greeted by a petite, black-haired lady, standing in the doorway. Her smile looked familiar. It seemed to be a combination of her own and the warm smile that her dad seldom showed, but that warmed her heart, over and over.

Her "G" had scooped her up. "Come on in here, Jasmine." Jasmine felt a bit nervous, but she walked into the house with her grandmother's arms still around her. I bet you are tired of sitting. "How long have you had my beautiful granddaughter cooped up in that car?" asked her "G".

Jasmine's dad replied, "It has been a while."

"Come on, honey. There is so much that I want to show you." her grandma cooed. Jasmine followed her grandmother through the house. It seemed that they exited one doorway, only to enter another. "Here is a surprise for you," her grandma stated. Looking down, Jasmine saw the most beautiful locket. She picked it up, nervously. "I have been saving this for you. It was your great granny's…my mom's." Jasmine pulled it closer for a better view.
"Let me put it on you, you beautiful girl."

8. Which of the following BEST describes Jasmine's location in this story?

Ⓐ At her home
Ⓑ At her daddy's house
Ⓒ At her friend's house
Ⓓ At her G's house

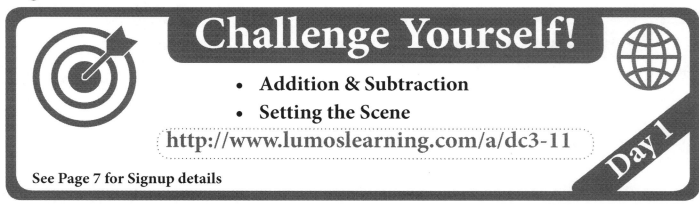

Challenge Yourself!

- **Addition & Subtraction**
- **Setting the Scene**

http://www.lumoslearning.com/a/dc3-11

Day 1

See Page 7 for Signup details

Day 2

1. Multiply:
6 x 10 = ____

Ⓐ 66
Ⓑ 60
Ⓒ 61
Ⓓ 16

2. What is the product of 10 and 10?

Ⓐ 20
Ⓑ 50
Ⓒ 100
Ⓓ 1,000

3. Find the product.
5 x 40 = _____

Ⓐ 100
Ⓑ 90
Ⓒ 200
Ⓓ 240

4. Match the multiplication expression with the correct product.

	630	320	540	450
9 x 60 =				
4 x 80 =				
90 x 5 =				
90 x 7 =				

The Blues

The Blues is a genre of music that can be directly traced to the "Deep South". The Blues were influenced by a mixture of traditional African music and Southern spirituals. The bedrock of the Blues is set in the Mississippi Delta, where many of the most influential Blues musicians were born. Many of these musicians are self-taught artists. This genre of music has influenced other music genres such as Rock and Roll, Rap, and Country.

One of the most famous Mississippi Delta Blues artists was a man named Robert Johnson. His ability to play the guitar has spawned numerous stories of his ability to play the guitar so well. No matter what story you choose to believe, it is undeniable that Mr. Johnson inspired many future artists with his unique playing style. So the next time you hear your favorite song, ask yourself if you believe that the Blues had some influence on that song.

5. According to the passage where was Robert Johnson from?

Ⓐ The passage does not state specifically where Robert Johnson was from.
Ⓑ Robert Johnson was from Chicago.
Ⓒ The passage states that Robert Johnson was from the Mississippi Delta.
Ⓓ Robert Johnson was from Africa.

6. Where did the Blues begin?

Ⓐ The Blues began in Africa.
Ⓑ The passage states that the Blues began in the Deep South.
Ⓒ The Blues began in Europe according to the passage.
Ⓓ The Blues began in the Northern states of the U.S.

7. What type of music does the passage say that the Blues has influenced?

Ⓐ The passage does not say that the blues have influenced any other type of music.
Ⓑ The passage states that the Blues have influenced Rock and Roll, Rap, and Country.
Ⓒ The passage says that the Blues have only influenced classical music.
Ⓓ The passage says that the Blues have only influenced guitar players.

Playing Video Games

Scotty loves to play video games! I mean he plays every chance he gets. He even plays when he should be doing his homework, chores or going to bed! It has gotten so bad that his parents are considering a punishment to teach him a lesson.

Scotty doesn't understand why they are upset with him and is trying to figure out what he can do so that he doesn't get his video game machine taken away. He has asked his friends for their ideas on the subject, too. He even asked his counselor at school. Scotty has been seeing her since his grades started dropping. The counselor told him it is very simple, give up the game playing on his own and get back to doing homework, chores, and going to bed on time.

To Scotty, the ideas his counselor told him are good, but he is very reluctant to do it. So one of his friends, Hailey, has offered to help. She is going to make him a chart of time spent on playing games compared to time spent on his responsibilities. He agrees to give it a try.

8. Who should Scotty share his chart with? Circle the correct answer choice.

(A)   His counselor
(B)   His parents
(C)   His friend, Hailey
(D)   All of the above

Challenge Yourself!

- **Multiplying Multiples of 10**
- **Explicitly Comprehension**

http://www.lumoslearning.com/a/dc3-12

Day 2

See Page 7 for Signup details

Day 3

Fractions of a Whole (3.NF.A.1)

1. What fraction of the letters in the word "READING" are vowels?

Ⓐ $\frac{4}{7}$

Ⓑ $\frac{3}{4}$

Ⓒ $\frac{3}{7}$

Ⓓ $\frac{1}{3}$

2. A bag contains 3 red, 2 yellow, and 5 blue tiles. What fraction of the tiles are below?

Ⓐ $\frac{2}{5}$

Ⓑ $\frac{2}{10}$

Ⓒ $\frac{3}{7}$

Ⓓ $\frac{1}{3}$

3. A rectangle is cut into four equal pieces. Each piece represents what fraction of the rectangle?

Ⓐ one half
Ⓑ one third
Ⓒ one fourth
Ⓓ one fifth

4. Which of the following fractions could apply to this figure? Select all correct answers.

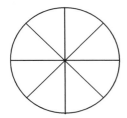

Ⓐ $\frac{1}{3}$

Ⓑ $\frac{1}{8}$

Ⓒ $\frac{1}{5}$

Ⓓ $\frac{8}{8}$

The Main Idea Arena (RI.3.2)

Day 3

Everything in nature follows a pattern. Circles, lines, spirals, and angles are repeated to make a design or a pattern. Patterns in nature are not just pretty adornments. They serve a purpose that has helped nature survive and flourish.

Have you ever taken a close look at a beehive? Well, not too close or you might get stung! The natural pattern in beehives is so perfect that it seems to be computer designed. The hives are made up of layers and layers of cells. Each cell has six perfectly equal sides or hexagons. Why would bees build six-sided cells, instead of round, or box shaped ones? The reason is because the bee is a genius at geometry and architecture! Six-sided cells use up every bit of space and allow bees to get the maximum area for storing honey. Also, Hexagons use the least honeycomb wax because all six sides are identical in length. The bees don't waste space, material, or effort. Aren't they smart insects?

5. What is the main idea of the selection?

Ⓐ Beehives have a disorganized pattern.
Ⓑ Every cell in the beehive has a different shape.
Ⓒ Every cell in the beehive has five sides.
Ⓓ Every thing in nature follows a pattern.

6. What is the above passage telling us?

Ⓐ It's introducing the reader to patterns.
Ⓑ It tells us how bees makes use of patterns.
Ⓒ It tells us how patterns are used only by people.
Ⓓ It tells us how bees have limited intelligence.

A robot is a device that can do tasks that are difficult or impossible for human beings. A robot does not have to be shaped like a person; robots can be shaped like animals or machines. Law enforcement agencies have robots that can go into dangerous areas, which might cause injury to individuals and thereby help in maintaining law and order with ease. Medical facilities have microscopic robot cameras that go into areas of the human body, robot cameras bloodstreams, that are too small for a doctor to see. Military units have robotic devices such as drone airplanes that can deliver bombs without risk to the soldiers who are operating the planes. Robots are also being sent into outer space to explore areas that are too dangerous for humans to visit.

7. What is the main idea in this passage?

Ⓐ Robots can be shaped like animals or machines.
Ⓑ A robot is a device that can do tasks that would be difficult or impossible for human beings.
Ⓒ Law enforcement, agencies have that robots can go into dangerous areas where a person could be injured.
Ⓓ A robot does not have to be shaped like a person.

Hobbies are Good for the Mind and Body

Many people enjoy hobbies. They can range from designing arts and crafts to singing in a choir. Hobbies improve self-esteem, physical well-being and can increase your academic gains, as well.

Arts and crafts have been known to enable you to gain higher fine motor skills while creating unique works of art. Learning how to work slowly and taking time to complete projects can help you to learn self- control, and develop patience. Some forms of arts and crafts include drawing, painting, building model cars, model airplanes, jewelry making, and leather work. There are many arts and craft stores where you can find your interests.

Sports have always been great hobbies for the young and old. Team and individual sports include football, baseball, soccer, swimming, tennis, wrestling and more. Quite often you join a sport to be with friends, learn to develop physical strength, or to enjoy what you like doing most. Communities generally have organizations to help parents and their children find the best sport for them.

Another form of hobbies includes collecting. You can start collecting sports cards, and comic books at an early age. Doll collections, kept in pristine condition over the years can even be a financial plus when you get older. Your parents and relatives can help you start your collection if you ask them to give you collectible items you want for birthday presents or other occasions.

Did you know that even the performing arts are considered a hobby? Joining a ballet class, drama club, tap and gymnastics, theatre or choir, can be your hobby. Again these types of hobbies help develop physical and emotional skills to improve your health and well-being.

8. Which is NOT the best way to summarize the selection about hobbies? Circle the correct answer choice.

Ⓒ Hobbies help you physically, emotionally, and can improve your life.

Ⓓ Hobbies can be fun and help you get along with others.

Ⓔ Hobbies include many things that people like to do.

Ⓕ Hobbies take a lot of time and can be expensive to do.

Challenge Yourself!

- **Fractions of a Whole**
- **The Main Idea Arena**

http://www.lumoslearning.com/a/dc3-13

Day 3

See Page 7 for Signup details

Day 4

1. What fraction does the number line show?

Ⓐ $\dfrac{1}{4}$

Ⓑ $\dfrac{1}{3}$

Ⓒ $\dfrac{3}{4}$

Ⓓ $\dfrac{4}{4}$

2. What fraction does the number line show?

Ⓐ $\dfrac{1}{2}$

Ⓑ $\dfrac{2}{2}$

Ⓒ $\dfrac{1}{3}$

Ⓓ $\dfrac{2}{3}$

3. What fraction does the number line show?

Ⓐ $\dfrac{2}{8}$ Ⓒ $\dfrac{3}{8}$

Ⓑ $\dfrac{3}{5}$ Ⓓ $\dfrac{4}{8}$

4. There are 3 number lines in the first column. Which fractions are represented by the dots on the number lines? For each number line, select the correct answer.

	4/4	8/9	5/8
Number line 1 (0 to 1)	○	○	○
Number line 2 (0 to 1)	○	○	○
Number line 3 (0 to 1)	○	○	○

Cause and Effect (RI.3.3)

Day 4

The Bluegrass State

There is one state with water, wildlife, and mountains. Does this sound too good to be true? Well, it isn't all of these natural features are in The Bluegrass State. These are some of the reasons that people visit Kentucky. Kentucky is home to wonderful lakes that offer fun water activities.

Cumberland Falls is a huge waterfall. It has been nicknamed "the Niagara of the South". If you are looking to do more than just see the water, a visit to beautiful Lake Cumberland might be a good stop for you. Here you can enjoy boating, fishing, or jet skiing. The Bluegrass State has a lot to offer for those looking for fun in the water.

Maybe, you are more of a wildlife person. Many people love hunting in the western part of the state. Natural wildlife can be found throughout the area. There are excursions in the Daniel Boone National Forest that are great also.

If this does not sound like fun to you, then you might like to learn more about Kentucky's horses. You can visit one of the race tracks or horse farms. Visitors from all over the world have visited Churchill Downs. Their horses race in the Kentucky Derby. Several other races that can be attended throughout the year. Other locations that allow you to enjoy Kentucky's best thoroughbreds include the Kentucky Horse Park and Keeneland.

Kentucky's tourism doesn't stop there. Guests can visit Mammoth Cave and the home of Abraham Lincoln. Certainly, the Bluegrass State is filled with features that keep people visiting this beautiful.

5. Which of the following probably happened BEFORE tourists started visiting Kentucky to see the exciting race horses?

Ⓐ Churchill Downs was built.
Ⓑ Lake Cumberland was developed.
Ⓒ The Daniel Boone National Forest was named.
Ⓓ The owners of Keeneland invited guests from all around the world.

Amelia Earhart

Amelia Earhart was born on July 24, 1897. She lived with her grandparents until the age of 12 when she and her sister went to live with their parents in 1909. Amelia's plans were to attend college, but when she came across four wounded World War I soldiers, she decided that she wanted to become a nurse. Her dedication to helping people led her from nursing to work as a social worker. While she worked as a social worker, she often spent her free time teaching immigrant children how to speak English.

Her most noteworthy journey began in 1920 when she took a ten-minute plane ride that completely changed her life. She decided to focus on earning a pilot's license. She challenged herself with a variety of jobs to earn the $1,000 needed for flying lessons to fulfil her dream.

Amelia Earhart proceeded to excel as a pilot. She received a medal from President Herbert Hoover in 1932 for her solo flight across the Atlantic. She did not stop there. Earhart was the first female to fly from Hawaii to California.

Amelia Earhart's contribution to history ended on July 2, 1937, when a frantic message was received by the U. S. Coast Guard. The message was from Earhart stating that she and the plane were in trouble. The plane went down, and no one has ever seen Earhart again. Her devotion to creating change remains a legacy. This legacy emphasizes how setting dreams and achieving goals can be done through hard work and determination.

6. Which sentence indicates why Earhart never went to college?

Ⓐ She lived with her grandparents until the age of 12 when she and her sister went to live with their parents in 1909.
Ⓑ Amelia's plans were to attend college, but when she came across four wounded World War I soldiers, she decided that she wanted to become a nurse.
Ⓒ Her dedication to helping people led her from nursing to work as a social worker, where she spent her free time teaching immigrant children the English language.
Ⓓ Her most noteworthy journey began in 1920 when she took a ten-minute plane ride that forever changed her life.

Cell Phones in the Classroom

A familiar ringtone sounds in the classroom directing everyone's attention to a shy student in the back row. Several years ago, this would have seemed a bit strange, but not today. A recent study showed that one in three third grade students have a cell phone. With so many students having access to technology devices, a lot of talks has gone into deciding whether to use them as learning tools or to ban them from the classroom.

Let's think cell phones role as learning tools. Annie needs a calculator, but forgot hers. She takes out her cell phone and is able to use the calculator app on the phone. Just across the room, Johnny is trying to spell the word "similar," so he uses the dictionary app on his phone to find the correct spelling. Mitchell, has completed all of his work early, so he decides to use the multiplication app on his phone to review multiplication facts in a fun and interactive way. These devices are causing teachers and other school officials see that cell phones give students access to resources that actually save schools money.

While cell phones may sound great, not every school district is ready to lift the cell phone ban. There are still those that have major concerns. One concern is what to do about students who do not have a cell phone. Another worry is how to make sure students are using the phone as a learning tool instead of texting and social media. Additional concerns arise with how to address when a phone is broken or stolen while at school. Certainly, the list of problems that some schools have goes on and on.

The answer isn't clear for schools across the United States. Some schools are starting to lift the cell phone ban, but others are keeping it in place. As students pack backpacks with cell phones, the discussion of having them in the classroom will certainly continue.

7. **What does the author state would be a positive effect of allowing students to have cell phones in the classroom?**

  Ⓐ   Students could access learning apps to assist in learning.
  Ⓑ   Students could stay in touch with their family and friends throughout the school by texting.
  Ⓒ   Students could stay connected through social media.
  Ⓓ   The school would have to buy students a new phone if their phone was broken or stolen while at school.

Read the passage and answer the question.

In 218 B.C., Romans ruled most of the world that they knew about. They felt protected by the Alps – high, snow-covered mountains to the east and north of them that enemies would find very difficult to cross. Then Hannibal came from Carthage, in what is now North Africa, with 9000 infantrymen – soldiers on foot – and something even more surprising: elephants. Hannibal had crossed the Alps with 37 elephants – creatures so terrifying that the Romans, who had never seen such animals, were thrown into a panic.

8. Based on what you know in this passage, what do you predict happened next?

Day 5

1. Which of these sets has the fractions listed from least to greatest?

Ⓐ $\frac{1}{6}, \frac{1}{4}, \frac{1}{3}, \frac{1}{2}$

Ⓑ $\frac{1}{2}, \frac{1}{3}, \frac{1}{6}, \frac{1}{4}$

Ⓒ $\frac{1}{3}, \frac{1}{4}, \frac{1}{2}, \frac{1}{6}$

Ⓓ $\frac{1}{2}, \frac{1}{3}, \frac{1}{4}, \frac{1}{6}$

2. Which of these fractions would be found between $\frac{1}{2}$ and 1 on a number line?

Ⓐ $\frac{1}{4}$

Ⓑ $\frac{1}{3}$

Ⓒ $\frac{5}{8}$

Ⓓ $\frac{3}{1}$

3. Which of these fractions would be found between 0 an $\frac{1}{2}$ on a number line?

Ⓐ $\frac{7}{8}$

Ⓑ $\frac{3}{4}$

Ⓒ $\frac{1}{4}$

Ⓓ $\frac{5}{8}$

4. Which of the following fractions is the least?

$$\frac{6}{5}, \frac{6}{4}, \frac{6}{10}, \frac{6}{9}.$$

Write your answer in the box below.

```
(                                    )
```

Educational Expressions (RI.3.4)

Day 5

Many animals in the wild eat other animals. These animals are called carnivores. Carnivores include lions, tigers, and bears.

5. What does carnivore mean in this paragraph?

- Ⓐ A plant eating animal
- Ⓑ An animal that eats plants and animals
- Ⓒ A meat eating animal
- Ⓓ An animal that eats dead

Clouds in the sky are able to produce rain. They get their water through evaporation. The sun heats the water in rivers, lakes, and even puddles, turning it into a vapor. Clouds are produced when lots of this vapor comes together.

6. What is evaporation?

- Ⓐ Water turning into rain
- Ⓑ Clouds making rain
- Ⓒ Water heating up and turning into a vapor
- Ⓓ Water being absorbed by clouds.

The world's population is growing every day! Thousands of babies are born each day, adding to the number of people on earth.

7. What does the underlined word mean?

- Ⓐ number of babies
- Ⓑ number of countries
- Ⓒ number of days
- Ⓓ number of people

Cell Phones in the Classroom

A familiar ringtone sounds out in the classroom directing everyone's attention to a shy student in the back row. Several years ago, this would have seemed a bit strange, but not today. A recent study showed that every one in three, third grade students, has a cell phone. With so many students having access to these technology devices, a lot of talks has gone into whether to use them as learning tools or keep them banned from the classroom.

Let's think about their role as learning tools. Annie needs a calculator, but forgot hers. She takes out her cell phone and is able to use the calculator app on the phone. Just across the room, Johnny is trying to spell the word "similar" so he uses the dictionary app on his phone to find the correct spelling. Another student in the class, Mitchell, has completed all of his work early, so he decides to use the multiplication app on his phone to review his multiplication facts in a fun and interactive way. These and other apps are making teachers and other school officials see that cell phones do give students access to many resources that could actually save schools money.

While cell phones may sound great, not everyone is ready to lift the cell phone ban. There are still those that have major concerns. One concern is what to do about students that do not have a cell phone. Another worry is how to make sure students are using the phone as a learning tool instead of texting and social media. Additional concerns arise with how to address when a phone is broken or stolen while at school. Certainly, the list of problems that some schools have goes on and on.

The answer isn't clear for schools across the United States. Some schools are starting to lift the cell phone ban, but others are keeping it in place. As more and more backpacks get armed with cell phones, the discussion of having them in the classroom will certainly continue into the future.

8. **What does the underlined word in the following sentence from the passage MOST LIKELY mean? Circle the correct answer choice.**

   These and other apps are making teachers and other school officials to see that cell phones do give students <u>access</u> to many resources that could actually save schools money.

   Ⓐ money
   Ⓑ a waste of time
   Ⓒ a block
   Ⓓ a connection

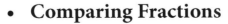

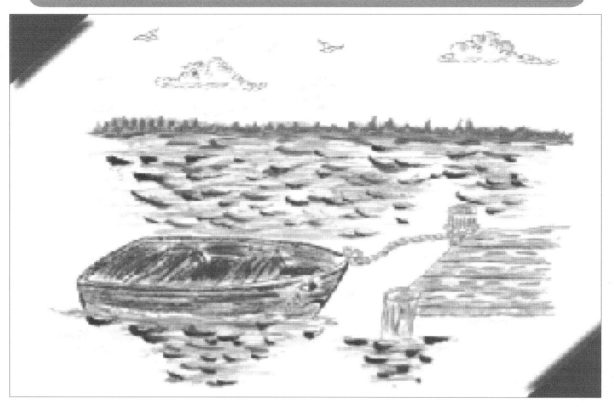

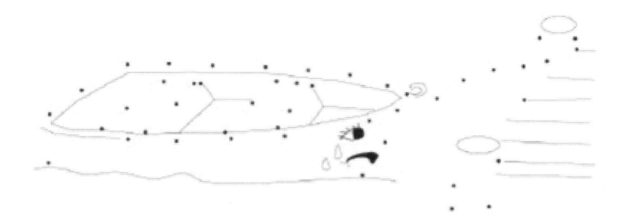

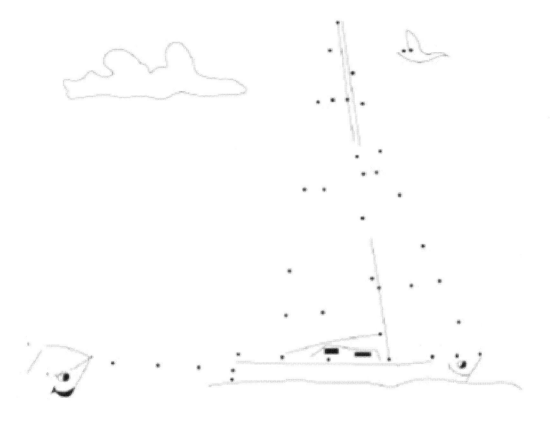

This Week's Online Activities

- **Reading Assignment**
- **Vocabulary Practice**
- **Write Your Summer Diary**

https://www.lumoslearning.com/a/slh3-4

See Page 7 for Signup details

Weekly Fun Summer Photo Contest

Take a picture of your summer fun activity and share it on Twitter or Instagram

Use the **#SummerLearning** mention

@LumosLearning on Twitter or

@lumos.learning on Instagram

Tag friends and increase your chances of winning the contest

Participate and stand a chance to WIN $50 Amazon gift card!

Telling Time (3.MD.A.1)

Day 1

1. What time does this clock show?

Ⓐ 3:12
Ⓑ 2:17
Ⓒ 2:22
Ⓓ 2:03

2. What time does this clock show?

Ⓐ 5:42
Ⓑ 9:28
Ⓒ 6:47
Ⓓ 5:47

3. What time does this clock show?

Ⓐ 10:00
Ⓑ 12:50
Ⓒ 10:02
Ⓓ 9:41

4. The clocks in the first column show different times. For each clock in the first column, select the correct answer.

	9:42	11:58	2:03
	○	○	○
	○	○	○
	○	○	○

Special Text Parts (RI.3.5)

Day 1

From McGuffey's Second Eclectic Reader

1.	There are three kinds of bees: workers, drones, and queens.
2.	Bees live in a house that is called a hive.
3.	Only one queen can live in each hive. If she is lost or dead, the other bees will stop their work.
4.	They are very wise and busy little creatures. They all join together to build cells of wax for their honey.
5.	Each bee takes its proper place, and does its own work. Some go out and gather honey from the flowers; others stay at home and work inside the hive.
6.	The cells which they build, are all one shape and size, and there are no spaces between them.

7.   The cells are not round, but have six sides.
8.   Have you ever looked into a glass hive to see the bees at work? They are always busy.
9.   The drones do not work. Every year before winter, all of the drones are driven from the hive or killed. The reason the drones are driven from the hive or killed is that they did not help make the honey, so the other bees do not allow them to eat the honey.
10.   It is not safe for children to handle bees because they have stingers. Bees use their stingers as a great defensive tool.

5. How does the author of this selection help the reader easily locate information?

Ⓐ By using a title
Ⓑ By using headers
Ⓒ By numbering the sentences
Ⓓ By organizing the sentences

6. Which sentence tells the reader about the jobs bees perform?

Ⓐ Sentence 3
Ⓑ Sentence 4
Ⓒ Sentence 6
Ⓓ Sentence 9

With junk food becoming increasingly popular, and families being on the go more than ever, kids and their parents need to know how to make healthier food choices. It is important that children learn to make healthy food choices from an early age. If children learn to make these choices, it not only makes them healthy, but also it keeps them in shape.

Staying in shape is one way of saying that someone makes wise decisions about eating, exercising and maintaining a healthy weight. Staying in shape not only helps your body to work well, but helps you feel better too. Who doesn't want to feel well to enjoy fun activities with others?

While parents are responsible for making wise choices too, there are many ways that kids can step up to the plate and take charge. Let's start by talking about the types of foods that kids should eat. Sure, daily food habits, not cake and ice cream. Your body needs a variety of healthy foods. By giving your body a lot of different foods, it will be able to get the nutrients that it needs. Don't be afraid to try new foods. You may not like everything that you try, but by trying new things, you will find more foods that you like. Throughout each day, try to eat five servings of fruits and vegetables. Hopefully, out of the five you will be able to find two fruits and three vegetables to enjoy.

Now, that we have looked at some wise food choices, let's take a look at what you should be drinking. Water and milk are always the best choices. There is nothing that quenches your thirst like a cold glass of water. Now, you may have often wonder why schools serve cartons of milk. The truth is, milk is needed to help build strong bones because it contains calcium. Kids younger than 9 years old should drink 2 cups of milk per day. If milk isn't your favorite thing to drink there are other ways to get the calcium that your body needs.

Some great dairy alternatives that introduce calcium into your diet are cheddar cheese and yogurt. You may be wondering if milk and water should be your only drink choices, and the answer is no. You can choose juice drinks that are 100% pure. This means that they are not loaded down with sugar. Many sodas, juice cocktails, and fruit punches have extraordinary amounts of sugar. Along with choosing the right foods and drinks, try to stay in shape with exercise.

It is important to try to find a way to be active for at least one hour daily. This might include playing basketball, riding a bike, or swimming. Now sometimes the weather won't allow you to enjoy these outdoor activities, so choose to get physical indoors by turning on some music that you enjoy and dancing to the beat. Other ideas include going bowling or turning your living room into a studio for "Simon Says" where you get to follow and give commands, such as: "Simon Says do 10 jumping jacks…." Just remember the idea is to get up and get active.

Staying fit doesn't have to be hard. It simply requires making wise choices. Try to make fruits, vegetables, milk, water, and exercise a part of your daily routine! You will feel great, and your body will thank you by giving you lots of energy to do the things that you most enjoy.

7. If the author of this passage wanted the reader to do additional research, what key word would BEST help them in their Internet search?

Ⓐ Jumping Jacks
Ⓑ Ways to Stay Healthy
Ⓒ Drinking Milk and Water
Ⓓ The Food Group

from McGuffey's Second Eclectic Reader
blos'soms drear'y wea'ry pinks smell'ing toil'ing
lev'ies buzz fra'grant this'tle weeds scent
treas'ure yel'low mead'ow tax sum'mer clo'ver
cloud'y dai'sy daf'fo dil lies columbine humming

8. This poem is meant to be read out loud. Why does the author use apostrophes (') in this selection?

Ⓐ To show the reader how to pronounce the words
Ⓑ To show the reader where the syllables divide in the words
Ⓒ To show the reader the meaning of each word
Ⓓ To show the reader how loudly to read the selection

Challenge Yourself!

- **Telling Time**
- **Special Text Parts**

http://www.lumoslearning.com/a/dc3-16

See Page 7 for Signup details

Day 1

Day 2

1. Cedric began reading his book at 9:12 AM. He finished at 10:02 AM. How long did it take him to read his book?

   Ⓐ 50 minutes
   Ⓑ 40 minutes
   Ⓒ 48 minutes
   Ⓓ 30 minutes

2. Samantha began eating her dinner at 7:11 PM and finished at 7:35 PM so that she could go to her room and play. How long did Samantha take to eat her dinner?

   Ⓐ 34 minutes
   Ⓑ 21 minutes
   Ⓒ 24 minutes
   Ⓓ 30 minutes

3. Tanya has after school tutoring from 3:00 PM until 3:25 PM. She began walking home at 3:31 PM and arrived at her house at 3:56 PM. How long did it take Tanya to walk home?

   Ⓐ 31 minutes
   Ⓑ 15 minutes
   Ⓒ 56 minutes
   Ⓓ 25 minutes

4. Tim went out for some work. He left home at 11:30 AM and returned back at 3:45 PM. How long was he away from home? Circle the correct answer.

   Ⓐ 3 hours and 15 minutes
   Ⓑ 4 hours and 15 minutes
   Ⓒ 3 hours and 45 minutes
   Ⓓ 4 hours and 45 minutes

What Did You Already Know? (RI.3.6)

Day 2

Everything in nature follows a pattern. Circles, lines, spirals, and angles are repeated to make a design or a pattern. Patterns in nature are not just pretty adornments. They serve a purpose that has helped nature survive and flourish.

Have you ever taken a close look at a beehive? Well, not too close or you might get stung! The natural pattern in beehives is so perfect that it seems to be computer designed. The hives are made up of layers and layers of cells. Each cell has six perfectly equal sides or hexagons. Why would bees build six-sided cells, instead of round, or box shaped ones? The reason is that the bee is a genius at geometry and architecture! Six-sided cells use up every bit of space and allow bees to get the maximum area for storing honey. Also, Hexagons use the least honeycomb wax because all six sides are identical in length. The bees don't waste space, material, or effort. Aren't they smart insects?

5. Where might a reader use the information about hexagons from this passage?

Ⓐ When solving a math problem on algebra.
Ⓑ When writing a math paper on geometric properties of a hexagon.
Ⓒ When building your home.
Ⓓ None of the above.

What is the most poisonous creature on earth? Many people guess that the answer would be a snake, a jellyfish, a scorpion, or a spider. Actually, most scientists agree that the most venomous animal is a harmless-looking small golden frog, called "teribilis." The golden frog is so toxic that even touching it can be dangerous to humans. A single frog contains enough poison to kill 20,000 mice or ten people.

6. What should you do if you see a teribilis? Write your answer in the box below

The Bluegrass State

There is one state with water, wildlife, and mountains. Does this sound too good to be true? Well, it isn't all of these natural features are in The Bluegrass State. These are some of the reasons that people visit Kentucky. Kentucky is home to wonderful lakes that offer fun water activities.

Cumberland Falls is a huge waterfall. It has been nicknamed "the Niagara of the South". If you are looking to do more than just see the water, a visit to beautiful Lake Cumberland might be a good stop for you. Here you can enjoy boating, fishing, or jet skiing. The Bluegrass State has a lot to offer for those looking for fun in the water.

Maybe, you are more of a wildlife person. Many people love hunting in the western part of the state. Natural wildlife can be found throughout the area. There are excursions in the Daniel Boone National Forest that are great also.

If this does not sound like fun to you, then you might like to learn more about Kentucky's horses. You can visit one of the race tracks or horse farms. Visitors from all over the world have visited Churchill Downs. Their horses race in the Kentucky Derby. Several other races that can be attended throughout the year. Other locations that allow you to enjoy Kentucky's best thoroughbreds include the Kentucky Horse Park and Keeneland.

Kentucky's tourism doesn't stop there. Guests can visit Mammoth Cave and the home of Abraham Lincoln. Certainly, the Bluegrass State is filled with features that keep people visiting this beautiful.

7. Based on the author's description of Kentucky, what type person might NOT enjoy visiting Kentucky?

- Ⓐ a hiker
- Ⓑ a horse lover
- Ⓒ a person who loves shopping
- Ⓓ a camper

PATTY AND THE SQUIRREL
from McGuffey's Second Eclectic Reader

1. Little Patty lives in a log house near a great forest. She has no sisters, and her big brothers are away all day helping their father.

2. But Patty is never lonely; for, though the nearest house is miles away, she has many little friends. There are two squirrels that live in the woods that are her friends.

3. How did Patty teach them to be so tame? Patty came to the woods often, and was always so quiet and gentle that the squirrels soon found they need not be afraid of her.

4. She brought her bread and milk to eat under the trees, and was sure to leave crumbs for the squirrels.

5. When they came near, she sat very still and watched them. So, little by little, she made them her friends, till, at last, they would sit on her shoulder, and eat from her hand.

6. Patty even helps the squirrels build their summer and winter homes. Their summer homes are made of leaves, and sticks, and moss. Their winter homes are found in hollow old trees.

7. Patty helps the squirrels and the squirrels help Patty not be lonely.

8. What do you think caused Patty to befriend the squirrels?

Challenge Yourself!

- **Elapsed Time**
- **What Did You Already Know?**

http://www.lumoslearning.com/a/dc3-17

See Page 7 for Signup details

Day 2

Day 3

1. "40 pounds" is printed at the bottom of a bag of sand. The number "40" is being used to _____ .

   Ⓐ count
   Ⓑ name
   Ⓒ locate
   Ⓓ measure

2. In the metric system, which is the best unit to measure the mass of a coffee table?

   Ⓐ Milliliters
   Ⓑ Kilograms
   Ⓒ Grams
   Ⓓ Liters

3. Which unit should be used to measure the amount of water in a small bowl?

   Ⓐ Cups
   Ⓑ Gallons
   Ⓒ Inches
   Ⓓ Tons

4. There are 8 water coolers in a school. Each water cooler holds 7 liters of water. All the water coolers were filled up in the morning. In the evening 5 liters of water remained. How much water was consumed? Explain how you got the answer in the box below.

Read the following sentence and view the map to answer the questions.

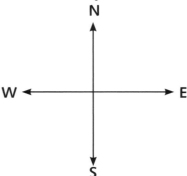

Elizabeth recently moved to Riverville. She is having a hard time finding her way around town.

5. What direction will Elizabeth have to travel in order to get to Mill Street?

- Ⓐ   South
- Ⓑ   East
- Ⓒ   North
- Ⓓ   There is not a Mill Street listed on this map.

6. If Elizabeth leaves River Street walking west what streets will she travel to get to the school?

- Ⓐ   Main, Oak, Pine, Maple, School
- Ⓑ   River, Hill, Grove, School
- Ⓒ   River, Maple, School
- Ⓓ   River, Maple, Lemon, Pine

Read the following information about our solar system. Use the illustration to help in answering the question.

There are eight named planets in our solar system. The planets orbit the sun at their own pace. Mercury takes the shortest amount of time to orbit the sun; it takes Mercury 87.969 days to make a complete trip around the sun. Neptune makes the longest journey around the sun. It takes this planet 60,190 days to make a trip around the sun. Neptune is the farthest planet from the sun; this is the reason for the extended travel time. Despite the placement of the planets each one has to orbit the sun.

Orbiting Times around the Sun

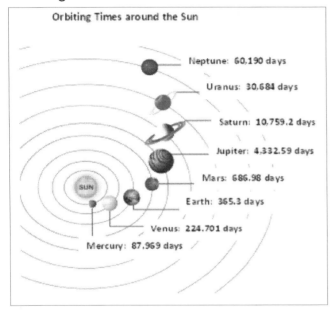

7. **Which planets take fewer days than Earth to orbit the sun?**

Ⓐ Mars, Jupiter, Saturn, Uranus, Neptune
Ⓑ Earth takes the fewest days to orbit the sun.
Ⓒ Venus and Mercury
Ⓓ Neptune and Uranus

Read the information passage about ice cream and view the timeline to answer the question.

The United States of America consumes more ice cream in one year than any other country. The average American eats forty-eight pints of ice cream a year. The most common flavor is vanilla. July has been deemed National Ice Cream Month in the United States. Since Americans love ice cream so much it might be important to examine the history of ice cream in the U.S.

Ice cream was first introduced in the United States in the 1700s. Only the wealthy could afford to buy it. The first widely seen advertisement for ice cream was circulated in 1777. The Ice cream industry began in Boston in 1851. The ice cream sundae was created in 1874. The first ice cream cone was in 1904 at the St. Louis World's Fair. Ice cream has become a popular treat for many Americans.

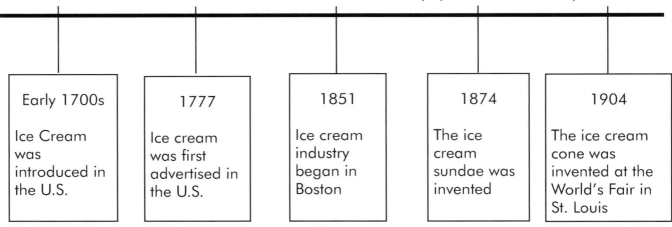

Early 1700s	1777	1851	1874	1904
Ice Cream was introduced in the U.S.	Ice cream was first advertised in the U.S.	Ice cream industry began in Boston	The ice cream sundae was invented	The ice cream cone was invented at the World's Fair in St. Louis

8. **In what year was ice cream first advertised in the United States?**
Circle the correct answer choice.

   Ⓐ 1904
   Ⓑ 1851
   Ⓒ Early 1700s
   Ⓓ 1777

Day 4

1.

Class Survey Should there be a field trip?		
	Yes	**No**
Mr. A's class	ЖЖ ЖЖ IIII	ЖЖ II
Mr. B's class	ЖЖ ЖЖ ЖЖ	ЖЖ ЖЖ III
Mr. C's class	ЖЖ ЖЖ I	ЖЖ ЖЖ I
Mr. D's class	ЖЖ ЖЖ II	ЖЖ ЖЖ

Four 3rd grade classes in Hill Elementary School were surveyed to find out if they wanted to go on a field trip at the end of the school year. The tally table above was used to record the votes.
How many kids voted "Yes" in Mrs. B's class?

Ⓐ 28 kids
Ⓑ 15 kids
Ⓒ 13 kids
Ⓓ 23 kids

2.

Should there be a field trip?		
	Yes	**No**
Mr. A's class	14	7
Mr. B's class	15	13
Mr. C's class	11	11
Mr. D's class	12	10
Total	52	41

Four 3rd grade classes in Hill Elementary School were surveyed to find out if they wanted to go on a field trip at the end of the school year. The table above shows the results of the survey.
How many kids voted "Yes" in Mr. A's class?

Ⓐ 7 kids
Ⓑ 15 kids
Ⓒ 14 kids
Ⓓ 21 kids

3.

Should there be a field trip?		
	Yes	No
Mr. A's class	14	7
Mr. B's class	15	13
Mr. C's class	11	11
Mr. D's class	12	10
Total	52	41

Four 3rd grade classes in Hill Elementary School were surveyed to find out if they wanted to go on a field trip at the end of the school year. The table above shows the results of the survey. How many kids altogether voted "No" for the field trip?

Ⓐ 82 kids
Ⓑ 11 kids
Ⓒ 52 kids
Ⓓ 41 kids

4. From the Venn Diagram given below, represent the number of people who only own cat as pet to the number of people who own only dog as a pet in the form of a fraction $\frac{a}{b}$

Pets We Have

Cat   Dog

Liz   Ryan
    Tim
Carly Ann   Joe

Will

The ostrich is the largest bird in the world, but it cannot fly. Its legs are so strong and long that it can travel faster by running. Ostriches use their wings to help them gather speed when they start to run. They also use them as brakes when they are turning and stopping.

Ostriches have been known to run at a rate of 96 km an hour. This is faster than horses can run, and as fast as most people drive a car. These huge birds stand as tall as a horse and sometimes weigh as much as 135 kg. In Africa, their home continent, they are often seen with large animals. The zebra, which is also a fast runner, seems to be one of their favorite companions.

Each ostrich egg weighs as much as two dozen chicken eggs. Ostrich eggs are delicious to eat and are often used as food in Africa. The shells also are made into cups and ornaments.

5. What is the author's opinion of the ostrich?

Ⓐ The author does not find it interesting.
Ⓑ The author finds the ostrich extraordinary.
Ⓒ The author likes ostrich eggs.
Ⓓ The author likes zebras.

Everything in nature follows a pattern. Circles, lines, spirals, and angles are repeated to make a pattern. Patterns in nature are not just pretty adornments. They serve a purpose that has helped nature survive and flourish. Have you ever taken a close look at a beehive? (Well, not too close or you might get stung!) The natural pattern in beehives is so perfect that it seems to be computer designed. The hives are made up of layers and layers of cells. Each cell has six perfectly equal sides. Why would bees build hexagonal cells, why not circular or box-shaped ones? The bee is a genius at geometry and architecture! Six-sided cells allow bees to get maximum space for storing honey. Hexagons also use the least building material because all six sides are common to other cells. The bees don't waste space, material or effort. Aren't they smart insects?

6. Based on the selection, what is likely to happen to you if you go near a beehive?

Ⓐ You will be stung.
Ⓑ You will eat honey.
Ⓒ You will be worried.
Ⓓ You will get hurt.

7. What can you conclude after reading this passage?

Ⓐ Hexagon shaped buildings use more building materials.
Ⓑ Bees are very smart insects.
Ⓒ Nothing in nature follows a pattern.
Ⓓ Bees are lazy.

It's the Twenty-First Century

With new times comes change. Allowing cell phones in classrooms is one type of change that I am talking about. So many kids have them, so why not let them be used for something good?

If we were allowed to use cell phones in class, we wouldn't have to always be waiting for the computer lab to open up. We can use our cell phones to do research.

Our teachers love showing us cool learning tools, but we never get to use them during the school day. Sometimes we forget about them before we go home. If we have our cell phones right there in class, we can use them then and not forget about what we are being shown.

Cell phones can also replace planners. They can allow us to keep track of important due dates for assignments, the days tests are scheduled, and other important reminders. Students lose their assignment books, but they will keep up with their cell phones.

I hope that I have shown you why having cell phones in the classroom is a great idea. This resource can benefit all of us. Let's lift that cell phone ban. After all, it is the twenty-first century.

8. What was the author's reason for writing this piece? Circle the correct answer choice.

- Ⓐ   To state an opinion
- Ⓑ   To narrate a memory
- Ⓒ   To inform about the history of cell phones
- Ⓓ   To entertain the reader with a fictional story

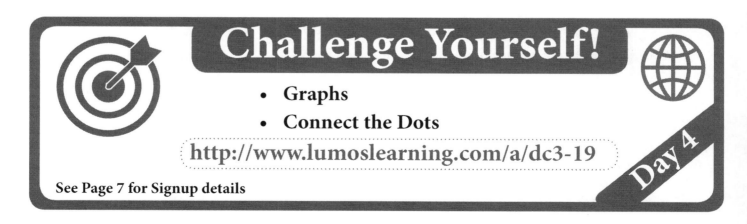

Challenge Yourself!
- **Graphs**
- **Connect the Dots**

http://www.lumoslearning.com/a/dc3-19

See Page 7 for Signup details

Day 4

Day 5

1. Which of these units is part of the metric system?

Ⓐ Foot
Ⓑ Mile
Ⓒ Kilometer
Ⓓ Yard

2. Which metric unit is closest in length to one yard?

Ⓐ decimeter
Ⓑ meter
Ⓒ millimeter
Ⓓ kilometer

3. Which of these is the best estimate for the length of a table?

Ⓐ 2 decimeters
Ⓑ 2 centimeters
Ⓒ 2 meters
Ⓓ 2 kilometers

4. Use the line plot to answer the questions given in the first column.

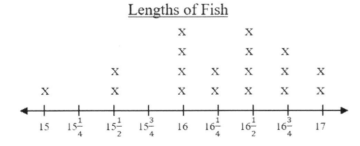

Lengths of Fish

Instruction:
X = 2 fishes

	4	6	8
How many fish are 16 $\frac{1}{2}$ inches long?	○	○	○
How many more fish are 16 inches long than 17 inches?	○	○	○
How many fish are less than 15 $\frac{3}{4}$ inches long?	○	○	○

Louisiana

It has been said that the state of Louisiana is a melting pot of people. Many different ethnic groups that have settled into pockets of this great state. Not only are there Vietnamese, Spanish, and Europeans, but there are also two unique ethnic groups. These two groups are the Cajuns and the Creoles.

The Cajuns are the French Canadians that moved down from Canada to Southern Louisiana. They fled Canada because of a British imposed rule that attempted to force all Canadians to accept the King's Protestant religion. Most of the French Canadians who moved to Louisiana were Catholics. When the Cajuns arrived in Louisiana they were accepted and allowed to practice any religion. As the Cajuns became more settled in Louisiana their customs and heritage began to impact the current populations' way of life. The Cajuns impact is still seen today throughout Louisiana.

Louisiana

The state of Louisiana has a mix of people from many different backgrounds. Many ethnic groups have settled into different parts of the state. There are people from Vietnam, Canada, and European countries that call this great state home. Additionally, there are two groups that moved into Louisiana many years ago. These two groups are the Creoles and Cajuns. It can be said these two groups of people have a blended set of backgrounds.

The Creoles are defined as any person who was born in New Orleans that has French or Spanish family roots. This includes anyone that comes from Africa, the Caribbean, France, or any Spanish country. The Creoles, like the Cajuns, have had a huge impact on the Louisiana lifestyle. Many of their traditions have contributed to Louisiana's unique art, music, and cooking. New Orleans is truly a different place to live and visit thanks to the Cajuns and the Creoles.

5. **From the two passages, which of the following answer choices explain a similarity between the Cajuns and the Creoles?**

   Ⓐ Cajuns and Creoles both moved to Louisiana from Canada.
   Ⓑ Both Cajuns and Creoles fled to Louisiana because they were Catholic and were not allowed to practice their religion in their home countries.
   Ⓒ All Cajuns and Creoles came from Spanish speaking countries.
   Ⓓ Both Cajuns and Creoles have impacted the Louisiana lifestyle.

6. **Which of the following answer choices accurately describe a difference in the two passages?**

   Ⓐ Cajuns fled Canada because they were not allowed to practice the Catholic religion.
   Creoles are people who live in New Orleans and are from French or Spanish family roots.
   Ⓑ Cajuns only live in New Orleans and Creoles live in only Southern Louisiana.
   Ⓒ There are no differences in Cajuns and Creoles because they are the same people.
   Ⓓ Cajuns are mainly from Africa while, Creoles are from Canada.

7. Which of the following answer choices accurately describe a key detail of these passages?

   Ⓐ A key point of these passages is that Louisiana offers many different types of food.
   Ⓑ A key point of these passages is that a lot of people have moved from Canada to Louisiana.
   Ⓒ A key point of these passages is that Cajuns and Creoles have impacted the Louisiana way of life.
   Ⓓ A key point of these passages is that you should visit Louisiana on your next vacation.

Picture Day

It is picture day at school and Sara is so excited. She is going to wear her new pink lace dress and shiny new black Mary Jane shoes. Sara's mom took extra time curling her hair this morning and even tied in a beautiful satin ribbon. Sara bound into the school feeling so pretty. She could hardly wait for her turn to get her picture taken.

Picture Day

Oh no! It's picture day at school. Melissa hates picture day, especially since her father lost his job. There is no money to buy a new dress, so she has to wear her sister's hand-me-downs. Melissa's mother tries to make her feel better by fixing her hair but nothing helps to change Melissa's mood. Melissa stomped into the school feeling ugly. Melissa was ready for this day to be over.

8. Which of the following answer choices describes a difference in the two passages?

   Ⓐ Both girls are excited about picture day at school.
   Ⓑ Sara is excited about picture day but Melissa is not excited about picture day.
   Ⓒ Both girls wore new dresses for picture day.
   Ⓓ The girls went to different schools.

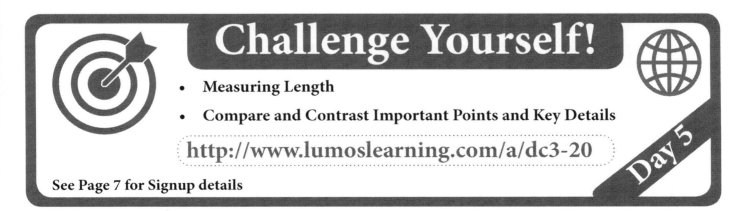

Challenge Yourself!

- **Measuring Length**

- **Compare and Contrast Important Points and Key Details**

http://www.lumoslearning.com/a/dc3-20

Day 5

See Page 7 for Signup details

Swimming: 7 Tips to Become a Better Swimmer

Just about everyone knows how to swim, or at least play around in the water. But you want to be a competitive swimmer, so how do you set yourself apart from all those people who just want to hang out at the pool? Here's a guide on how to take it to the next level.

1. Make Time for Practice

The best swimmers spend the most amount of time in the pool practicing their technique. While natural ability gives some people an advantage, the great ones are the ones who keep practicing.

Set aside time each day for some sort of swimming activity or exercise that you can do. Even if you don't have access to a pool every day, there's tons of exercises and drills that you can do to build strength and endurance. Make a plan and stick to it.

2. Know Your Sport

Freestyle swimming is the most common and well-known forms of swimming. A stroke is the full circle motion your arm makes when swimming. A freestyle stroke can be broken down into four phases. Those phases are catch, pull, exit, and recovery.

The catch phase is when your hand goes out in front of you and hits the water. In the pull phase, your hand goes underwater and down toward the bottom of the pool. In this phase, you are "pulling" yourself through the water. The exit phase is when your hand is coming up from the bottom of the pull phase. Your hand comes up from the bottom and comes up beside your leg. In the recovery phase, your arm is out of the water and rotates back towards the catch.

3. Improve Each Phase of the Stroke

Try swimming with your hand closed during the catch and pull phases. This will increase your forearm strength and help improve your stroke.

During the exit phase, flick your wrist at the end before it comes out of the water.

During the recovery phase, focus on getting your hand and arm back in the water as quickly as possible. The longer your hand is out of the water, the less time you spend pulling yourself forward.

4. Build Your Strength

To improve your swimming ability, you will need to improve your strength. Body weight exercises can be done anywhere and aren't likely to cause injury like weight lifting can.

Exercises like pushups and pull-ups strengthen your upper body. Doing these exercises will help you when you are pulling through the water.

Lunges, squats, and calf raises strengthen your lower body. These exercises will help you when you are kicking your legs, giving you more speed through the water.

Core exercises focus on your stomach, sides, lower back, and hips. Exercises such as crunches, leg raises, and bicycle kicks give your core a great workout. Strengthening your core will help you keep great form throughout your swim.

5. Increase Your Endurance

Even when you aren't in the pool, you can keep active to improve your endurance. Endurance exercises like biking and running help build your lung capacity so you can swim longer. Sprinting will help build muscle endurance so you can swim faster and harder without getting tired.

6. Breathing

It is important to learn to breathe correctly when swimming. New swimmers have a habit of bringing their head out of the water and breathing through their mouth.

Instead of bringing your head all the way out of the water, take breaths through your nose as you turn your head to the side. Practice this technique in shallow water without swimming, then try it while swimming.

7. Find a Good Coach.

Even the most successful athletes have coaches. A good coach can set you up with an exercise program. The coach also gets to see you swim on a regular basis. That way she can tell you what you might be doing wrong and help correct it.

And most importantly, remember to have fun!

This Week's Online Activities

- Reading Assignment
- Vocabulary Practice
- Write Your Summer Diary

https://www.lumoslearning.com/a/slh3-4

See Page 7 for Signup details

Weekly Fun Summer Photo Contest

Take a picture of your summer fun activity and share it on Twitter or Instagram

Use the **#SummerLearning** mention

@LumosLearning on Twitter or

@lumos.learning on Instagram

Tag friends and increase your chances of winning the contest

Participate and stand a chance to WIN $50 Amazon gift card!

Week 5 Summer Practice

Day 1

1. The area of a plane figure is measured in _____ units.

   (A) cubic
   (B) meter
   (C) square
   (D) box

2. Which of these objects has an area of about 1 square inch?

   (A) a sheet of writing paper
   (B) a beach towel
   (C) a dollar bill
   (D) a postage stamp

3. Mr. Parker wants to cover a mural with cloth. The mural is 12 inches long and 20 inches wide. How many square inches of cloth does Mr. Parker need?

   (A) 240 square inches
   (B) 32 square inches
   (C) 120 square inches
   (D) 220 square inches

4. The area of a rectangle A is 75 sq. cm. The area of square B is one third the area of the rectangle A. What is the side length of the square B? Circle the correct answer.

   (A) 7 cm
   (B) 5 cm
   (C) 4 cm
   (D) 6 cm

Day 1

5. What is the plural form of the word baby?

  Ⓐ babys
  Ⓑ babies
  Ⓒ babes
  Ⓓ babeys

6. What is the plural of day?

  Ⓐ days
  Ⓑ daies
  Ⓒ daes
  Ⓓ day

7. What is the plural form of butterfly?

8. All of the children were happy when their grandmother and aunt came to visit last Sunday.

  Which of the words from this sentence is NOT a noun? Circle the correct answer choice.

  Ⓐ children
  Ⓑ happy
  Ⓒ aunt
  Ⓓ Sunday

Challenge Yourself!

- **Area**
- **People, Places, and Things**

 http://www.lumoslearning.com/a/dc3-21

Day 1

See Page 7 for Signup details

1. Find the area of the object below.

3 feet

29 feet

- Ⓐ   87 square feet
- Ⓑ   32 square feet
- Ⓒ   64 square feet
- Ⓓ   128 square feet

2. Find the area of the object below.

12 yards

15 yards

- Ⓐ   108 square yards
- Ⓑ   54 square yards
- Ⓒ   27 square yards
- Ⓓ   180 square yards

3. How could the area of this figure be calculated?

33 inches

63 inches

- Ⓐ   Multiply 63 x 33 x 63 x 33
- Ⓑ   Add 63 + 33 + 63 + 33
- Ⓒ   Multiply 63 x 33
- Ⓓ   Multiply 2 x 63 x 33

4. **Seth wants to cover his table top with a piece of fabric. His table is 2 meters long and 4 meters wide. How much fabric does Seth need?**

Ⓐ 6 square meters
Ⓑ 10 square meters
Ⓒ 8 square meters
Ⓓ 16 square meters

Replace Those Nouns (L.3.1.A)

Day 2

5. **A noun is a word that is the name of a person, place, or thing. What is a noun in the sentence below?**

Charlene is the best forward on the team this season.

Ⓐ is
Ⓑ team
Ⓒ this
Ⓓ on

6. **A pronoun is a word that takes the place of a noun. What are the pronouns in the sentence below?**

Alice helped Jim with homework, and when he gave her a gift, she loved it.

7. **When will Monica find out where** _____ **new school will be?**

What pronoun best fits in the blank?

Ⓐ Jamie's
Ⓑ her
Ⓒ she
Ⓓ his

8. Choose the pronoun that best completes the following sentence.

_____ brought me a bouquet of flowers last week.

Ⓐ They
Ⓑ We
Ⓒ Us
Ⓓ She and I

Challenge Yourself!

- **Relating Area to Addition & Multiplication**
- **Replace Those Nouns**

http://www.lumoslearning.com/a/dc3-22

Day 2

See Page 7 for Signup details

Day 3

1. What is meant by the "perimeter" of a shape?

Ⓐ The distance from the center of a plane figure to its edge
Ⓑ The distance from one corner of a plane figure to an opposite corner
Ⓒ The distance around the outside of a plane figure
Ⓓ The amount of space covered by a plane figure

2. Complete the following statement.
Two measurements associated with plane figures are _____.

Ⓐ perimeter and volume
Ⓑ perimeter and area
Ⓒ volume and area
Ⓓ weight and volume

3.

This rectangle is 4 units long and one unit wide. What is its perimeter?

Ⓐ 10 units
Ⓑ 4 units
Ⓒ 5 units
Ⓓ 8 units

4. The perimeters of the rectangles are given in the first column. For each perimeter, select the possible areas of the rectangles.

Note that for each perimeter, more than one option may be correct.
Instruction: Assume that the length and the width of the rectangles are whole numbers.

	15 sq. cm.	10 sq. cm.	12 sq. cm.
Perimeter = 16 cm	☐	☐	☐
Perimeter = 14 cm	☐	☐	☐
Perimeter = 22 cm	☐	☐	☐

5. Which of the following answer choices is an example of a plural noun written correctly?

Ⓐ childrens
Ⓑ mice
Ⓒ doctores
Ⓓ womans

6. Which of the following words in the sentence below is an example of a plural noun?

We saw four deer in the field on our hiking trip.

Ⓐ we
Ⓑ four
Ⓒ our
Ⓓ deer

7. Which answer choice demonstrates the correct plural spelling for the word "berry"?

Ⓐ berry
Ⓑ berries
Ⓒ berrys
Ⓓ berryes

8. Which of the following words is incorrectly transformed from the plural form to its singular form?

Ⓐ Countries = Country
Ⓑ Dwarfs = Dwarf
Ⓒ Wifes = Wife
Ⓓ Moose = Moose

Challenge Yourself!

- Perimeter
- Regular & Irregular Plural Nouns

http://www.lumoslearning.com/a/dc3-23

Day 3

See Page 7 for Signup details

Day 4

1. **Fill in the blank with the correct term.**
   Closed, plane figures that have straight sides are called _____ .

   Ⓐ parallelograms
   Ⓑ line segments
   Ⓒ polygons
   Ⓓ squares

2. **Which of the following shapes is not a polygon?**

   Ⓐ Square
   Ⓑ Hexagon
   Ⓒ Circle
   Ⓓ Pentagon

3. **Complete this statement.**
   A rectangle must have _____ .

   Ⓐ four right angles
   Ⓑ four straight angles
   Ⓒ four obtuse angles
   Ⓓ four acute angles

4. **Which of the following figures have at least one set parallel sides? Note that more than one option may be correct.**

   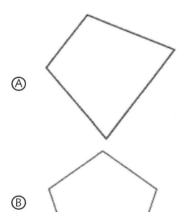
   Ⓐ

   Ⓑ

   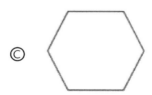
   Ⓒ

   Ⓓ

5. Which word in the following sentence is an abstract noun?

The crime was committed on the corner of Jackson Avenue and Main Street.

Ⓐ committed
Ⓑ avenue
Ⓒ crime
Ⓓ corner

6. Which word in the following saying is an abstract noun?

"Beauty is in the eye of the beholder."

Ⓐ beauty
Ⓑ eye
Ⓒ in
Ⓓ the

7. Which of the following is an example of an abstract noun?

Ⓐ dog
Ⓑ wisdom
Ⓒ apartment
Ⓓ teacher

8. Which of the following words in the sentence below is an example of an abstract noun?

The teacher used treats as motivation to encourage her students to increase their reading levels.

Challenge Yourself!

- 2-Dimensional Shapes
- Awesome Abstract Nouns

http://www.lumoslearning.com/a/dc3-24

Day 4

See Page 7 for Signup details

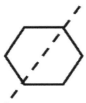

Day 5

1. What is the dotted line that divides a shape into two equal parts called?

Ⓐ   a middle line
Ⓑ   a line of symmetry
Ⓒ   a line of congruency
Ⓓ   a divider

2. A square has how many lines of symmetry?

Ⓐ   8
Ⓑ   4
Ⓒ   1
Ⓓ   2

3. Which of the following has NO lines of symmetry?

Ⓐ

Ⓑ

Ⓒ

Ⓓ

4. A circle has an area of 96 sq. cm. The circle is divided into 8 equal parts. Which of the following statements are correct? Select all the correct answers.

Ⓐ   If you shade 3 parts, the area of the shaded portion is 32 sq. cm.
Ⓑ   If you shade 4 parts, the area of the shaded portion is 48 sq. cm.
Ⓒ   If you shade 7 parts, the area of the shaded portion is 84 sq. cm.
Ⓓ   If you shade 2 parts, the area of the shaded portion is 24 sq. cm.

Show Me the Action (L.3.1.D)

Day 5

5. Choose the correct form of the action word given below and fill in the blank.
The bear was _____ angrily.

Ⓐ growl
Ⓑ growled
Ⓒ growling
Ⓓ growls

6. Choose the correct form of the action word given below and fill in the blank.
The monkey was _____ on the branch of the tree.

Ⓐ sleep
Ⓑ slept
Ⓒ sleeps
Ⓓ sleeping

7. Choose the following word that correctly completes the sentence.
I often _____ into the woods to be with nature.

Ⓐ wonder
Ⓑ wander
Ⓒ yonder
Ⓓ ponder

8. How would this sentence be written if it happened yesterday?
I drink three glasses of milk every day.
Circle the correct answer choice

Ⓐ I drinked three glasses of milk yesterday.
Ⓑ I drank three glasses of milk yesterday.
Ⓒ I will drink three glasses of milk yesterday.
Ⓓ I drink three glasses of milk yesterday.

Challenge Yourself!

- **Shape Partitions**
- **Show Me the Action**

http://www.lumoslearning.com/a/dc3-25

Day 5

See Page 7 for Signup details

Maze Game

MAZE GAME

Help Santa Claus find the Christmas tree

MAZE GAME

Help fox find mushroom

MAZE GAME

Help fox find mushroom

MAZE GAME

Help squirrel find acorn

This Week's Online Activities

- **Reading Assignment**
- **Vocabulary Practice**
- **Write Your Summer Diary**

https://www.lumoslearning.com/a/slh3-4

See Page 7 for Signup details

Weekly Fun Summer Photo Contest

Take a picture of your summer fun activity and share it on Twitter or Instagram

Use the **#SummerLearning** mention

@LumosLearning on Twitter or

@lumos.learning on Instagram

Tag friends and increase your chances of winning the contest

Participate and stand a chance to WIN $50 Amazon gift card!

Day 1

1. Which number sentence describes this array?

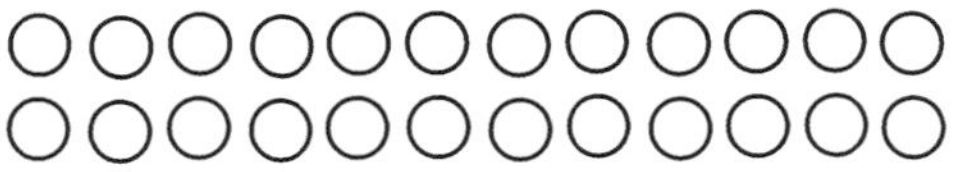

○○○○○○○○○○○○
○○○○○○○○○○○○

Ⓐ 2 x 12 = 24
Ⓑ 2 + 12 = 14
Ⓒ 12 + 2 = 24
Ⓓ 10 x 2 = 20

2. Identify the multiplication sentence for the picture below:

Ⓐ 4 x 4 = 16
Ⓑ 4 x 3 = 12
Ⓒ 3 x 4 = 12
Ⓓ 4 x 2 = 8

3. What multiplication fact does this picture model?

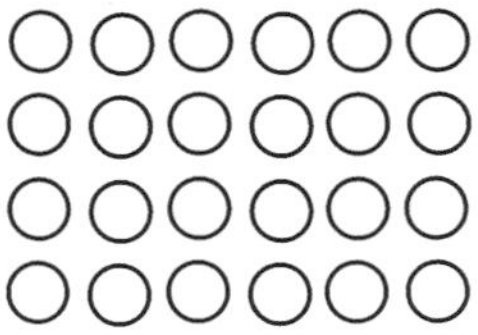

○○○○○○
○○○○○○
○○○○○○
○○○○○○

Ⓐ 4 x 6 = 24
Ⓑ 4 x 7 = 28
Ⓒ 6 x 3 = 18
Ⓓ 7 x 4 = 28

4. PART A

John finds the solution for 8 x 6 by solving for (8 x 5) + 8. Is John correct? Explain why you think that John's strategy is correct or not? Write your answer in the box below.

PART B

There are Seven boys, and each of them buys 6 pens. How many pens do they buy all together? Write an equation to represent this. Also, Find the total number of pens purchased using the equation.

5. What is the past tense form of the verb "play"?

Ⓐ plays
Ⓑ played
Ⓒ will play
Ⓓ playing

6. Which verb tense is the underlined word in the sentence below?

Jason will try to come to the party tomorrow.

Ⓐ present
Ⓑ past
Ⓒ future

7. Which of the following verbs is an example of a present tense verb?

Ⓐ speaks
Ⓑ jumped
Ⓒ will sing
Ⓓ driven

8. What is the present tense of the underlined verb in the following sentence?

We <u>rode</u> the merry-go-round at the mall five times.

Challenge Yourself!

- **Understanding Multiplication**
- **Simply Simple Verb Tenses**

http://www.lumoslearning.com/a/dc3-26

Day 1

See Page 7 for Signup details

Day 2

1. Jennifer picked 30 oranges from the basket. If it takes 6 oranges to make a one liter jar of juice, how many one liter jars of juice can Jennifer make?

   Ⓐ 4 jars
   Ⓑ 3 jars
   Ⓒ 6 jars
   Ⓓ 5 jars

2. Miller bought 80 rolls of paper towels. If there are 10 rolls of paper towels in each pack, how many packs of paper towels did Miller buy?

   Ⓐ 6 packs
   Ⓑ 8 packs
   Ⓒ 7 packs
   Ⓓ 5 packs

3. James takes 15 photographs of his school building. He gave the same number of photographs to 5 friends. How many photographs did James give to each friend?

   Ⓐ 2 photographs
   Ⓑ 3 photographs
   Ⓒ 6 photographs
   Ⓓ 5 photographs

4. Gabriela has a 16 stickers. She wants to find two ways to divide the stickers into equal groups. Which expressions can she use to divide the stickers? Mark all the correct answers.

   Ⓐ $16 \div 2$
   Ⓑ $16 \div 3$
   Ⓒ $16 \div 4$
   Ⓓ $16 \div 5$

Day 2

5. **Which sentence uses a subject and verb that agree?**

Ⓐ My sister always help my mother.
Ⓑ My sister always helping my mother.
Ⓒ My sister always helps my mother.
Ⓓ My sister always am helping my mother.

6. **Which sentence uses a subject and verb that agree?**

Ⓐ My neighbor and his dogs walks every day.
Ⓑ My neighbor and his dog walk every day.
Ⓒ My neighbor and his dog walking every day.
Ⓓ My neighbor and his dog do walks every day.

7. **What form of the underlined verb agrees with the subject in this sentence?**

My sister and her friend <u>goes</u> to the park.

Ⓐ goes
Ⓑ going
Ⓒ go
Ⓓ goed

8. **Fill in the blank with the correct verb form**

Eating these foods _____ her more energy for the race.

Challenge Yourself!

* **Understanding Division**
* **Make It Make Sense**

http://www.lumoslearning.com/a/dc3-27

Day 2

See Page 7 for Signup details

1. Jonathan can do 7 jumping jacks. Marcus can do 4 times as many as Jonathan. How many jumping jacks can Marcus do?

   Ⓐ 28
   Ⓑ 8
   Ⓒ 4
   Ⓓ 7

2. Darren has seen 4 movies this year. Marsha has seen 3 times as many movies as Darren. How many movies has Marsha seen?

   Ⓐ 7
   Ⓑ 3
   Ⓒ 4
   Ⓓ 12

3. Sarah is planting a garden. She will plant 4 rows with 9 seeds in each row. How many plants will be in the garden?

   Ⓐ 32 seeds
   Ⓑ 36 seeds
   Ⓒ 42 seeds
   Ⓓ 13 seeds

4. **PART A**
   Fill in the blank with the correct symbol to make this equation true.

   $64 \div 8 = 2$ ___ $4.$

   PART B
   Fill in the blank with the correct symbol to make this equation true.

   2 ___ $4 = 42 \div 7.$

Day 3

5. Bears are so 'growly' means that _____.

Ⓐ bears roar
Ⓑ bears shout
Ⓒ bears growl
Ⓓ bears howl

6. Fill in the blanks with the correct descriptive word.

Giraffes have _____ necks.

Ⓐ longer
Ⓑ long
Ⓒ elongate
Ⓓ short

7. An adjective is a word that describes a noun or pronoun. What is the adjective in the sentence below?

The assignment was confusing, so I didn't do it.

Ⓐ assignment
Ⓑ confusing
Ⓒ I
Ⓓ do

8. Choose the word that is acting as an adverb in the following sentence.

Her behavior only mildly disrupted the actors.

Challenge Yourself!

- **Applying Multiplication & Division**
- **Tell Me More**

http://www.lumoslearning.com/a/dc3-28

Day 3

See Page 7 for Signup details

Day 4

Finding Unknown Values (3.OA.A.4)

1. **Find the number that makes this equation true.**
   n ÷ 9 = 8

   Ⓐ n = 81
   Ⓑ n = 45
   Ⓒ n = 72
   Ⓓ n = 63

2. **Find the number that makes this equation true.**
   ____ ÷ 3 = 10

   Ⓐ 27
   Ⓑ 30
   Ⓒ 33
   Ⓓ 60

3. **Find the number that makes this equation true.**
   45 ÷ n = 9

   Ⓐ n = 10
   Ⓑ n = 7
   Ⓒ n = 5
   Ⓓ n = 3

4. **Enter the correct answer in the table.**

Equation	Product
4 x 8=	
	x 7 = 63
3 x 5=	
	x 1 =7

5. Is the underlined conjunction in the sentence below an example of a coordinating or subordinating conjunction?

We will be going shopping today <u>rather than</u> going shopping on Saturday.

Ⓐ coordinating
Ⓑ subordinating

6. What word in the following sentence is an example of a subordinating conjunction?

Francis was watching television until her friend Maris came over.

Ⓐ watching
Ⓑ was
Ⓒ came
Ⓓ until

7. What is the correct definition of a coordinating conjunction?

Ⓐ a conjunction that links words, phrases, and clauses that have equal importance.
Ⓑ a conjunction that introduces a coordinating clause.
Ⓒ a conjunction that introduces a subordinating clause.
Ⓓ a conjunction that shows the action that the subject is doing in a sentence.

8. What is the coordinating conjunction in the following sentence?

My mom cooked spaghetti for dinner but I really wanted lasagna.

Challenge Yourself!

- **Finding Unknown Values**
- **Subordinating and Coordinating Conjunctions**

http://www.lumoslearning.com/a/dc3-29

Day 4

See Page 7 for Signup details

Day 5

1. Which two numerical expressions both have a value of 0?

   Ⓐ 60 x 1 and 1 x 60
   Ⓑ 10 x 10 and 0 x 10
   Ⓒ 27 x 0 and 0 x 27
   Ⓓ 0 ÷ 15 and 15 ÷ 15

2. Which mathematical property does this equation model?
   6 x 1 = 6

   Ⓐ Commutative Property of Multiplication
   Ⓑ Associative Property of Multiplication
   Ⓒ Identity Property of Multiplication
   Ⓓ Distributive Property

3. Which mathematical property does this equation model?
   9 x 6 = 6 x 9

   Ⓐ Commutative Property of Multiplication
   Ⓑ Associative Property of Multiplication
   Ⓒ Identity Property of Multiplication
   Ⓓ Distributive Property

4. **(2 x 3) x 4 = 24 and 2 x (3 x 4) = 24**

   Identify the property that is applicable. Circle the correct answer choice.

   Ⓐ Associative property of multiplication
   Ⓑ Distributive property
   Ⓒ Commutative property of multiplication
   Ⓓ Identity Property of Multiplication

5. Giraffes are long-legged and meek.
What type of sentence is this?

Ⓐ Descriptive (paints a picture in the reader's mind)
Ⓑ Informative
Ⓒ Interrogative (asks a question)
Ⓓ Imperative (states a command or makes a request)

6. Sammy likes to play soccer, and he also likes to play basketball.
What type of sentence is this?

Ⓐ simple
Ⓑ compound
Ⓒ Complex

7. When I eat too much candy, I get a stomach ache.

What type of sentence is this?

Ⓐ simple
Ⓑ compound
Ⓒ complex

8. Choose the word that BEST completes the following sentence.
Alexander forgot his glasses on the counter _____ his mom was able to bring them to school for him.

Ⓐ ,and
Ⓑ ,but
Ⓒ ,so
Ⓓ ,like

Challenge Yourself!

- **Multiplication & Division Properties**
- **Mix Up Those Sentences**

http://www.lumoslearning.com/a/dc3-30

Day 5

See Page 7 for Signup details

This Week's Online Activities

- **Reading Assignment**
- **Vocabulary Practice**
- **Write Your Summer Diary**

https://www.lumoslearning.com/a/slh3-4

See Page 7 for Signup details

Weekly Fun Summer Photo Contest

Take a picture of your summer fun activity and share it on Twitter or Instagram

Use the **#SummerLearning** mention

@LumosLearning on Twitter or

@lumos.learning on Instagram

Tag friends and increase your chances of winning the contest

Participate and stand a chance to WIN $50 Amazon gift card!

Day 1

Relating Multiplication & Division (3.OA.B.6)

1. Find the number that would complete both of the following number sentences.

   $50 \div$ ____ $= 5$
   ____ $\times 5 = 50$

   Ⓐ 15
   Ⓑ 5
   Ⓒ 45
   Ⓓ 10

2. Find the number that would complete both of the following number sentences.

   $36 \div$ ____ $= 9$
   ____ $\times 9 = 36$

   Ⓐ 4
   Ⓑ 5
   Ⓒ 27
   Ⓓ 9

3. There are 9 students in a group. Each student needs 5 sheets of paper to complete a project. Which number sentence below can be used to find out how many total sheets of paper are needed for this project?

   Ⓐ $45 \times$ ____ $= 9$
   Ⓑ $9 \times 45 =$ ____
   Ⓒ ____ $\div 5 = 9$
   Ⓓ $9 \div 5 =$ ____

4. Which number sentence is equivalent to the number sentence below:

   $65 \div n = 5.$

   Ⓐ $65 = 5 \times n$
   Ⓑ $65 = 5 \div n$
   Ⓒ $65 = n \div 5$
   Ⓓ $65 = 5 - n$

   Write your answer in the box given below.

5. Which word needs to be capitalized in this sentence?
   i called my mom to come and pick me up when i got sick at school.

   Ⓐ i
   Ⓑ my
   Ⓒ mom
   Ⓓ me

6. Which sentence has correct capitalization?

   Ⓐ i said, "i don't feel well, mom."
   Ⓑ I said, "i don't feel well, mom."
   Ⓒ I said, "I don't feel well, mom."
   Ⓓ I said, "I don't feel well, Mom."

7. Which sentence has correct capitalization?

   Ⓐ She said, "doctor, my child doesn't feel well."
   Ⓑ She said, "Doctor, my child doesn't feel well."
   Ⓒ She said, "Doctor, my Child doesn't feel well."
   Ⓓ She said, "Doctor, My Child doesn't feel well."

8. Read the book titles and make a tick mark in the column "Correct" or "Not Correct" as applicable.

	Correct	Not Correct
Little House on the Prairie		
A Wrinkle in Time		
The Lion King		
The Call of the Wild		

Challenge Yourself!

- Relating Multiplication & Division
- Capitalization Dedication

http://www.lumoslearning.com/a/dc3-31

Day 1

See Page 7 for Signup details

1. Solve.
   ___ = 5 x 9

   Ⓐ   40
   Ⓑ   45
   Ⓒ   50
   Ⓓ   35

2. Find the product of 8 and 6.

   Ⓐ   14
   Ⓑ   42
   Ⓒ   48
   Ⓓ   56

3. Find the product of 7 and 7.

   Ⓐ   42
   Ⓑ   46
   Ⓒ   49
   Ⓓ   56

4. Find the quotient. 27 ÷ 9 = ? Circle the correct answer.

   Ⓐ   18
   Ⓑ   4
   Ⓒ   3
   Ⓓ   2

5. Which address has correct punctuation?

Ⓐ 1345 Sycamore, Street Chicago IL 123452
Ⓑ 1345 Sycamore Street Chicago, IL 123452
Ⓒ 1345 Sycamore Street Chicago, IL, 123452
Ⓓ 1345 Sycamore, Street Chicago, IL, 123452

6. Which address has correct punctuation?

Ⓐ 8142 Brown, Avenue New York NY 14353
Ⓑ 8142 Brown, Avenue New York, NY 14353
Ⓒ 8142 Brown Avenue New York, NY 14353
Ⓓ 8142 Brown Avenue New York, NY, 14353

7. Which address has correct punctuation?

Ⓐ 800 Heartbreak Lane Las Vegas, NV 83902
Ⓑ 800 Heartbreak Lane Las Vegas, NV, 83902
Ⓒ 800 Heartbreak, Lane Las Vegas, NV 83902
Ⓓ 800 Heartbreak, Lane Las Vegas, NV, 83902

8. Jamie screamed, There is a spider.

Punctuate the sentence correctly and write it in the box below.

Day 3

1. George started with 2 bags of 10 cookies. He gave 12 cookies to his parents. How many cookies does George have now?

   Ⓐ 8 cookies
   Ⓑ 10 cookies
   Ⓒ 12 cookies
   Ⓓ 20 cookies

2. Renae has 60 minutes to do her chores and do her homework. She has 3 chores to complete and each chore takes 15 minutes to complete. After completing her chores, how many minutes does Renae have left to do her homework?

   Ⓐ 15 minutes
   Ⓑ 45 minutes
   Ⓒ 30 minutes
   Ⓓ 0 minutes

3. Anna and Jamie want to buy a new board game. The original cost was 28 dollars. It is on sale for 4 dollars off. How much money should each girl pay if they buy the game on sale and pay equal amounts?

   Ⓐ $24
   Ⓑ $2
   Ⓒ $12
   Ⓓ $14

4. For each of the problems in the first column, select the correct answer.

	$50	$5	$10	$4
Karen had 86 dollars. He bought 7 books. After buying them he had 16 dollars. How much did each book cost ?	○	○	○	○
Jose and his four friends bought a new board game. It was on sale for 20 dollars off. If each of the boys (total 5 of them) paid $6. What was the original cost of the new board game?	○	○	○	○
A shopkeeper buys 5 pens for $35 and sells them at the rate of $8 per pen. If he sells all the five pens, how much profit he will get?	○	○	○	○
Jeffrey bought 8 actions figures which cost 3 dollars each from John. John bought 6 books from the amount he received from Jeffrey. If the cost of each book John purchased is the same, what is the cost of each book?	○	○	○	○

5. Which of the following answers correctly uses a comma and quotation marks?

Ⓐ "Did you find the ball, asked Thomas "if not I will look for it too."
Ⓑ Elizabeth, shouted I hate my little brother"
Ⓒ Grant asked, "Can I have some more pizza?"
Ⓓ "She said I hope, it snows tomorrow."

6. Which of the following answers correctly uses a comma and quotation marks?

Ⓐ "Amber said," we need to go to the movies on Sunday.
Ⓑ Perry asked, "Are you going to be at the meeting tonight?"
Ⓒ "He replied," "I want a computer for my birthday."
Ⓓ "Let's visit the neighbors tomorrow instead of today suggested, Sammie."

7. Which of the following answers correctly uses a comma and quotation marks?

"There will be a math test tomorrow," stated Mr. Thompson.
"there will be a math test tomorrow stated Mr. Thompson."
"There will be a math test tomorrow. Stated Mr. Thompson.
"There will be a math test tomorrow. stated" Mr. Thompson.

8. Which of the following answers correctly uses commas and quotation marks? Choose the correct answer from the options given below by circling it.

Ⓐ "Bring me your papers said Mr. Golf, I need to grade them."
Ⓑ "Bring me your papers, said Mr. Golf I need to grade them."
Ⓒ "Bring me your papers said Mr. Golf I need to grade them."
Ⓓ "Bring me your papers," said Mr. Golf, "I need to grade them."

Challenge Yourself!

- **Two-Step Problems**
- **The Comma and Quotation Dilemma**

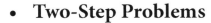

http://www.lumoslearning.com/a/dc3-33

Day 3

See Page 7 for Signup details

Day 4

1. Complete the following statement.
   The product of two even numbers will always be _____ .

   Ⓐ even
   Ⓑ odd
   Ⓒ a multiple of 10
   Ⓓ a square number

2. Complete the following statement.
   A number has a nine in its ones place. The number must be a multiple of _____.

   Ⓐ 9
   Ⓑ 3
   Ⓒ 7
   Ⓓ None of the above

3. Complete the following statement.
   Numbers that are multiples of 8 are all _____.

   Ⓐ even
   Ⓑ multiples of 2
   Ⓒ multiples of 4
   Ⓓ All of the above

4. Complete the following statement. **If you subtract an odd number from an even number, the difference will always be (a/an) _____. Circle the correct answer.**

   Ⓐ Multiple of 3
   Ⓑ Even number
   Ⓒ Odd number
   Ⓓ Odd number or Even number

5. Which word best completes the following sentence?

My things are all _____.

Ⓐ me's
Ⓑ I's
Ⓒ mine
Ⓓ I

6. Which pronoun best completes the following sentence?

Lydia's things are _____.

Ⓐ mine
Ⓑ yours
Ⓒ his
Ⓓ hers

7. Which pronoun best completes the following sentence?

Billy and Tim's things are _____.

Ⓐ mine
Ⓑ his
Ⓒ hers
Ⓓ theirs

8. Choose the sentence that is written ENTIRELY correctly.

Ⓐ We sent her a dozen roses to the hospital's.
Ⓑ She is going to need a lot of medicine to get better was the doctors words.
Ⓒ These paper's are getting wet in the rain.
Ⓓ I forgot to invite Julian to my party.

Challenge Yourself!

- **Number Patterns**
- **Impressive Possessives**

http://www.lumoslearning.com/a/dc3-34

Day 4

See Page 7 for Signup details

1. Round 2,564 to the nearest hundred.

Ⓐ 2,000
Ⓑ 2,500
Ⓒ 2,600
Ⓓ 2,700

2. Round 1,043 to the nearest hundred.

Ⓐ 1,000
Ⓑ 1,100
Ⓒ 1,040
Ⓓ 1,200

3. Round 537 to the nearest ten.

Ⓐ 500
Ⓑ 540
Ⓒ 550
Ⓓ 530

4. Round 489 to the nearest hundred. Write the correct answer into the box.

5. Which word is spelled correctly?

- Ⓐ hitchiker
- Ⓑ granddaughter
- Ⓒ naturaly
- Ⓓ mispelled

6. Which word is misspelled?

- Ⓐ hiker
- Ⓑ driver
- Ⓒ writer
- Ⓓ ridder

7. Which word is misspelled?

- Ⓐ field
- Ⓑ chief
- Ⓒ niece
- Ⓓ theif

8. Which word in the following sentence is misspelled? Write the word in the box given below

Please write the date on the board: Febuary 8, 2012.

 **Challenge Yourself!**

- **Rounding Numbers**
- **Compelling Spelling**

 http://www.lumoslearning.com/a/dc3-35

See Page 7 for Signup details

Day 5

Cross Word Puzzles

DOWN

ACROS

1. Cat 2. Cow 3. Duck 4. Chicken
5. Goat 6. Rooster 7. Turkey 8. Horse
9. Pig 10. Dog 11. Sheep

Answer: COUNTRYSIDE

This Week's Online Activities

- **Reading Assignment**
- **Vocabulary Practice**
- **Write Your Summer Diary**

https://www.lumoslearning.com/a/slh3-4

See Page 7 for Signup details

Weekly Fun Summer Photo Contest

Take a picture of your summer fun activity and share it on Twitter or Instagram

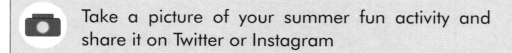

Use the **#SummerLearning** mention

@LumosLearning on Twitter or

@lumos.learning on Instagram

Tag friends and increase your chances of winning the contest

Participate and stand a chance to WIN $50 Amazon gift card!

Week 8 Summer Practice

Day 1

Addition & Subtraction (3.NBT.A.2)

1. Which of these expressions has the same difference as 94 - 50?

Ⓐ 70 - 34
Ⓑ 80 - 46
Ⓒ 60 - 16
Ⓓ 90 - 54

2. Which of these number sentences is not true?

Ⓐ 88 + 12 = 90 + 10
Ⓑ 82 + 18 = 88 + 12
Ⓒ 56 + 45 = 54 + 56
Ⓓ 46 + 15 = 56 + 5

3. Jim has 640 baseball cards and 280 basketball cards. How many sports cards does Jim have in all?

Ⓐ 820 cards
Ⓑ 360 cards
Ⓒ 8,120 cards
Ⓓ 920 cards

4. Hannah received a score of 604 on the exam. Ben received a score of 719. What was the difference between the two scores? Write your answer in the box given below.

5. How many syllables are in the word telescope?

An astronomer used to go out every night to observe stars. He would often be seen with a telescope in one hand and a notebook in the other.

Ⓐ one
Ⓑ two
Ⓒ three
Ⓓ four

6. How many syllables are in the word astronomer?

An astronomer used to go out every night to observe stars. He would often be seen with a telescope in one hand and a notebook in the other.

Ⓐ one
Ⓑ two
Ⓒ three
Ⓓ four

7. Which of the words in the following sentence has FOUR syllables?

I cannot attend your graduation party.

Ⓐ cannot
Ⓑ attend
Ⓒ graduation
Ⓓ party

8. How many syllables are in the word ostrich?

The ostrich is the largest bird in the world, but it cannot fly.

Challenge Yourself!

- **Addition & Subtraction**
- **Syllable Patterns**

http://www.lumoslearning.com/a/dc3-36

See Page 7 for Signup details

Day 1

Day 2

1. Multiply:
_____ = 6 x 60

- Ⓐ 120
- Ⓑ 180
- Ⓒ 320
- Ⓓ 360

2. Find the product of 70 and 7.

- Ⓐ 77
- Ⓑ 140
- Ⓒ 420
- Ⓓ 490

3. Multiply:
_____ = 30 x 7

- Ⓐ 210
- Ⓑ 240
- Ⓒ 180
- Ⓓ 100

4. Complete the following table:

a x b =	c
6 x 50 =	
8 x 60 =	
70 x 8 =	
80 x 9 =	

The teacher asked students in her class to write a research paper on the American Civil War. She also asked the students to list all sources of information on their papers. Nia, a student, went to the library and read books on the history of United States of America, and a book on the history of the American Civil War.

5. Where else can Nia get information for her paper?

Ⓐ A fashion magazine
Ⓑ A program on Civil War aired on the History Channel
Ⓒ A book on the history of Europe
Ⓓ A book on the Constitution of United States of America

6. What other sources would be most helpful for Nia to use to help her write her research paper?

Ⓐ Internet search on facts about the Civil War in the United States
Ⓑ Read a fiction story about the Civil War
Ⓒ Get ideas by reading about the civil war of another country
Ⓓ Interview the school principal

Beautiful seashells that are washed ashore on beaches by ocean waves have always fascinated human beings. Shells come in a wonderful array of shapes, sizes, and colors. Shells are actually made by marine creatures to serve as their homes.

7. If you were asked to do further research on seashells, where would you look for more information?

Look at the information provided in the three boxes below. Then, choose the answer choice that best answers each question.

#1	#2	#3
Wander - to move around with no specific destination	wander - synonyms: leave, walk, onward	Area: amount of space inside a shape
width - measurement from side to side.	width - synonyms: side, breadth	Length: measurement from top to bottom
wrist - a body part located between one's hand and forearm.	wrap - synonyms - cover, conceal	Width: measurement from side to side
yield - to pause.	wrist - synonyms: body part, arm	
	yield - synonyms: pause, stop	

8. Which box would contain a synonym for the word "Conceal"?

Ⓐ   Box # 1
Ⓑ   Box # 2
Ⓒ   Box # 3

Challenge Yourself!

- **Multiplying Multiples of 10**
- **What's Your Reference Preference**

http://www.lumoslearning.com/a/dc3-37

Day 2

See Page 7 for Signup details

1. What fraction of the square is shaded?

Ⓐ $\dfrac{1}{2}$

Ⓑ $\dfrac{1}{3}$

Ⓒ $\dfrac{2}{1}$

Ⓓ $\dfrac{1}{1}$

2. What fraction of the square is shaded?

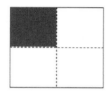

Ⓐ $\dfrac{1}{2}$

Ⓑ $\dfrac{1}{4}$

Ⓒ $\dfrac{1}{3}$

Ⓓ $\dfrac{3}{1}$

3. What fraction is NOT shaded?

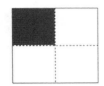

Ⓐ $\dfrac{1}{2}$

Ⓑ $\dfrac{1}{4}$

Ⓒ $\dfrac{3}{1}$

Ⓓ $\dfrac{3}{4}$

4. What fraction does each figure show? Write your answers in the blank boxes.

	Figure	Fraction
A		
B		
C		

Marina knew it would be a long time before she saw her mother's face again. When her grandmother asked her if she wanted to go on a two-week cruise to Alaska, Marina wasn't sure how to answer. Marina loved spending time with her grandma, but she had never been away from her mother and father for more than one night. Marina was sure that she would feel _____ because she couldn't see her parents for so long.

5. Which word best fills in the blank that will clearly show Marina's feelings at this point in the passage?

Ⓐ happy
Ⓑ concerned
Ⓒ sad
Ⓓ confused

I was ready for the competition this time. Last year during the kite flying competition, I was nervous and unprepared. I forgot my kite string and I had to borrow one from the judges. Once I got my kite into the air, I didn't do a very good job of controlling it, and it crashed into another kite. The two kites were tangled together, and the other flier and I were disqualified from the competition. This year was _____. I checked my kite for tears. It was perfect. I checked to make sure that the kite string was tied to the kite tightly, and that it was wound around the handle neatly.

6. Which word best fills in the blank that clearly completes the writer's thought?

Ⓐ different
Ⓑ the same
Ⓒ cloudy
Ⓓ nervous

Fauntleroy wanted to be as _____ a dragon, as his father. He had learned from an early age that dragons were meant to destroy things. His father was a fire-breather and had burned down many villages. Fauntleroy wanted to be just as dangerous and destructive as his father.

7. Which word best fills in the blank to tell what kind of dragon Fauntleroy dreams of becoming?

Ⓐ friendly
Ⓑ ferocious
Ⓒ large
Ⓓ fiery

8. Choose the word(s) that BEST completes a title for a speech that Mrs. Smith is giving to her third grade students.

Eating Healthy is _____

Ⓐ Gross
Ⓑ Rewarding
Ⓒ Costly
Ⓓ Not My Thing

Challenge Yourself!

- **Fractions of a Whole**
- **Connect the Word for Effect**

http://www.lumoslearning.com/a/dc3-38

Day 3

See Page 7 for Signup details

Day 4

1. **What fraction does the number line show?**

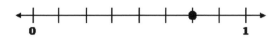

- Ⓐ $\dfrac{3}{8}$

- Ⓑ $\dfrac{6}{8}$

- Ⓒ $\dfrac{5}{8}$

- Ⓓ $\dfrac{4}{8}$

2. **What fraction does the number line show?**

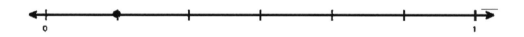

- Ⓐ $\dfrac{1}{6}$

- Ⓑ $\dfrac{4}{6}$

- Ⓒ $\dfrac{3}{6}$

- Ⓓ $\dfrac{1}{5}$

3. What fraction does the number line show?

Ⓐ $\dfrac{2}{4}$

Ⓑ $\dfrac{2}{3}$

Ⓒ $\dfrac{1}{3}$

Ⓓ $\dfrac{1}{4}$

4. Draw a number line and locate the fraction $\dfrac{5}{7}$ on it.

5. **Which of the following answer choices would be the correct way to write a sentence that would clarify the dialogue below?**

That dessert was a killer.

Ⓐ That dessert committed murder.
Ⓑ That dessert was excellent.
Ⓒ That dessert almost killed me.
Ⓓ That dessert was awful.

6. **If you were asked to verbalize the sentence below, what might you say?**

Jameson was out of touch about the story of the air plane crash.

Ⓐ Jameson was clueless.
Ⓑ Jameson is stupid.
Ⓒ Jameson knew some facts about the plane crash.
Ⓓ Jameson knows everything.

7. **If someone says "it's in the bag", what are they saying?**

Ⓐ You have something in a sack.
Ⓑ You found the item in a bag.
Ⓒ A situation has been solved or completed.
Ⓓ You have lost something.

8. **What sentence describes something as "grungy"?**

Ⓐ Kenny's clothes are always so clean.
Ⓑ Sara's dog always smells so good.
Ⓒ Peter and Pam have a nice new car.
Ⓓ James had on a pair of really dirty pants at school.

Challenge Yourself!

- **Fractions on the Number Line**
- **Differences in Spoken and Written Language**

http://www.lumoslearning.com/a/dc3-39

See Page 7 for Signup details

Day 4

Day 5

1. Which of these fractions would be found between 0 and $\frac{3}{4}$ on a number line?

   Ⓐ $\frac{7}{8}$

   Ⓑ $\frac{4}{8}$

   Ⓒ $\frac{5}{6}$

   Ⓓ $\frac{4}{4}$

2. Which of these fractions is less than $\frac{6}{8}$ = ?

   Ⓐ $\frac{1}{8}$

   Ⓑ $\frac{7}{8}$

   Ⓒ $\frac{9}{8}$

   Ⓓ $\frac{8}{8}$

3. Answer the following $\frac{1}{2}$ > _____

   Ⓐ $\frac{1}{4}$

   Ⓑ $\frac{2}{3}$

   Ⓒ $\frac{4}{8}$

   Ⓓ $\frac{2}{2}$

4. Which of these fractions is greater than $\frac{5}{7}$? Circle the correct answer.

(A) $\frac{1}{7}$

(B) $\frac{2}{7}$

(C) $\frac{4}{7}$

(D) $\frac{6}{7}$

Context Clue Crew (L.3.4.A)

Day 5

5. Which word means "time of day after the morning, but before the night"?

(A) afternoon
(B) noonafter
(C) aftermoon
(D) dawn

Amy, Ingrid, and Rebecca were friends. They went to school together. They had to cross a river on the way to school. The only way that they could cross it was by walking on a narrow tree trunk.

6. In the above paragraph, what is the meaning of the word "narrow"?

(A) the size of a bus
(B) very large
(C) not so wide
(D) the size of a car

Amy and her friends were off to school as usual. As they were crossing the narrow bridge, Rebecca, who was right in the back of the line, slipped on the narrow bridge. She gave a frightened scream, clutching hold of Ingrid who was in front of her. Both of them lost their balance and fell into the river. Amy clutched her mother in fright. For a moment, she hesitated and then threw herself into the river after her friends, determined to save them.

7. Which of the following words has the same meaning as "frightened"?

Ⓐ afraid
Ⓑ brave
Ⓒ strong
Ⓓ timid

[1]Maria is a very intelligent third grade student at Sunshine Elementary. [2]She is a <u>diligent</u> worker that wants to make straight A's. [3]Last night; she had a plethora of homework that took her several hours to finish. [4]She had two pages of math homework to complete. [5]She had a spelling worksheet. [6]She had a page of science homework. [7]She had one page of social studies homework to complete. [8]Her parents understand that she attends one of the top schools in the state and this requires a lot of hard work. [9]However, they feel that this amount of work is a bit absurd. [10]There is no time for their daughter's extracurricular activities. [11]They are going to call the school later today to discuss their concerns.

8. What does the underlined word in sentence 2 (diligent) MOST LIKELY mean?
Write your answer in the box given below.

Challenge Yourself!

- **Comparing Fractions**
- **Context Clue Crew**

http://www.lumoslearning.com/a/dc3-40

Day 5

See Page 7 for Signup details

This Week's Online Activities

- **Reading Assignment**
- **Vocabulary Practice**
- **Write Your Summer Diary**

https://www.lumoslearning.com/a/slh3-4

See Page 7 for Signup details

Weekly Fun Summer Photo Contest

Take a picture of your summer fun activity and share it on Twitter or Instagram

Use the **#SummerLearning** mention

@LumosLearning on Twitter or

@lumos.learning on Instagram

Tag friends and increase your chances of winning the contest

Participate and stand a chance to WIN $50 Amazon gift card!

Week 9 Summer Practice

Day 1

1. **What time does this clock show?**

   Ⓐ 12:39
   Ⓑ 8:04
   Ⓒ 1:38
   Ⓓ 12:42

2. **On an analog clock, the shorter hand shows the _____ .**

   Ⓐ minutes
   Ⓑ hours
   Ⓒ seconds
   Ⓓ days

3. **On an analog clock, the longer hand shows the _____ .**

   Ⓐ minutes
   Ⓑ hours
   Ⓒ days
   Ⓓ seconds

4. **John starts working in the garden at 5:30 PM and finishes 40 minutes later. What time does the clock show when John finishes his work? Represent this on a number line.**

5. What is the prefix in the word *bewailed*?

Ⓐ be-
Ⓑ bew-
Ⓒ -ed
Ⓓ wail

6. What is a *telescope*?

Ⓐ An instrument that helps us to see small objects by making them look bigger
Ⓑ An instrument that helps us to get a closer view of objects far away
Ⓒ An instrument that helps us to measure speed of a vehicle
Ⓓ An instrument that helps us to keep things cold and preserve them

7. Which part of the word *treatment* is a suffix?

Ⓐ -ment
Ⓑ treat-
Ⓒ trea-
Ⓓ -atment

8. Write the Prefix, Root word and Suffix in the correct order for the word "Disagreeable" in the boxes given below.

Prefix	Root Word	Suffix

Challenge Yourself!

- **Telling Time**
- **The Root & Affix Institute**

http://www.lumoslearning.com/a/dc3-41

Day 1

See Page 7 for Signup details

Day 2

1. **Doug loves to play video games. He started playing at 4:00 PM and did not finish until 5:27 PM. How long did Doug play video games?**

   Ⓐ 1 hour and 37 minutes
   Ⓑ 1 hour and 27 minutes
   Ⓒ 27 minutes
   Ⓓ 2 hours and 27 minutes

2. **Kelly has to clean her room before going to bed. She began cleaning her room at 6:12 PM. When she finished, it was 7:15 PM. How long did it take Kelly to clean her room?**

   Ⓐ 57 minutes
   Ⓑ 53 minutes
   Ⓒ 1 hour and 3 minutes
   Ⓓ 1 hour and 15 minutes

3. **Holly had a busy day. She attended a play from 7:06 PM until 8:13 PM. Then she went to dinner from 8:30 to 9:30 PM. How long did Holly attend the play?**

   Ⓐ 57 minutes
   Ⓑ 2 hours and 27 minutes
   Ⓒ 46 minutes
   Ⓓ 1 hour and 7 minutes

4. **Observe the two clocks. How many minutes have passed between the time shown in the first clock to the time in the second clock. Write your answer in the box given below.**

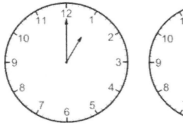 

View the dictionary excerpt and answer the question.
Main Entry: wrap
Pronunciation: 'rap
Function: verb

1 (a): to cover especially by winding or folding (b): to and secure for transportation or storage : BUNDLE (c) : ENFOLD, EMBRACE (d): to coil, fold, draw, or twine (as string or cloth) around something
2 a : to involve completely : ENGROSS
3 : to conceal or obscure as if by enveloping
4 : to finish filming or videotaping <wrap a movie>

5. Which definition of the word wrap is used in the sentence below?

Jenny was so wrapped up in the movie that she did not hear the phone ringing.

Ⓐ to envelop and secure for transportation or storage
Ⓑ to involve completely: ENGROSS
Ⓒ to conceal or obscure as if by enveloping
Ⓓ to finish filming or videotaping

6. Which of the following definitions best describes "strange".

The strange sound was coming from the basement door as we walked down the hall.

Ⓐ of, relating to, or characteristic of another country
Ⓑ not before known, heard, or seen
Ⓒ ill at ease
Ⓓ having the major characteristic of strangeness

Use the excerpt from a glossary found in a math book to answer the following question.

Addend: any number being added
A.M.: Times between 12:00 (midnight) and 12:00 (noon)
Area: A measurement of square units of the inside of a plane figure.
Array: The arrangement of objects that are in equal rows.
Bar graph: Is a graph that uses rectangles to compare the amounts of data.

7. Which of the words from the glossary is an example of a measurement of time?

Ⓐ bar graph
Ⓑ array
Ⓒ a.m.
Ⓓ Area

View the dictionary excerpt and answer the question.
Main Entry: **fan•cy**
Pronunciation: 'fan(t)-sE
Function: transitive verb
Inflected Form(s): **fan•cied; fan•cy•ing**
1 : to have a fancy for : **LIKE**
2 : to form a conception of : **IMAGINE** <fancy our embarrassment>
3 a : to believe mistakenly or without evidence b : to believe without being certain <she fancied she had met him before>
4 : to visualize or interpret as <fancied myself a child again>
synonym see **THINK**

8. Which definition states that fancy can mean to interpret as?

Ⓐ 2: to form a conception of
Ⓑ 1: to have a fancy for: Like
Ⓒ 4: to visualize or interpret as
Ⓓ 3b: to believe without being certain

Day 3

1. **Which unit in the customary system is best suited to measure the weight of a coffee table?**

   Ⓐ   Gallons
   Ⓑ   Pounds
   Ⓒ   Quarts
   Ⓓ   Ounces

2. **Which of these units could be used to measure the capacity of a container?**

   Ⓐ   pints
   Ⓑ   feet
   Ⓒ   pounds
   Ⓓ   millimeters

3. **Which of these is a unit of mass?**

   Ⓐ   liter
   Ⓑ   meter
   Ⓒ   gram
   Ⓓ   degree

4. **Circle the tool that should be used to measure a small amount of sugar.**

  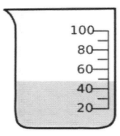

Day 3

5. Which list of words rhyme?

   Ⓐ toil, boil, soil
   Ⓑ soil, bail, tail
   Ⓒ twin, win, swing
   Ⓓ song, hung, sung

6. What word is a synonym for anxiously?

Maria waited anxiously for the concert to begin.

   Ⓐ unfriendly
   Ⓑ uneasily
   Ⓒ easily
   Ⓓ happily

7. What word is an antonym for the bold word in the sentence?

He couldn't believe his luck. "Ha! Ha!" he **laughed**.

   Ⓐ happy
   Ⓑ unhappy
   Ⓒ cried
   Ⓓ giggled

8. What is the antonym of the word "Carefully"? Write your answer in the box below.

Challenge Yourself!

- **Liquid Volume & Mass**
- **Making Words Work**

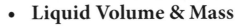

http://www.lumoslearning.com/a/dc3-43

See Page 7 for Signup details

Day 3

Day 4

1. The students in Mr. Donovan's class were surveyed to find out their favorite school subjects. The results are shown in the pictograph. Use the pictograph to answer the following question: How many students chose either science or math?

Our Favourite Subjects

Math	○ ○ ○ ○
Reading	○ ○
Science	○ ○ ○
History	○
Other	○ ○

Key: ○ = 2 votes

- Ⓐ 6 students
- Ⓑ 7 students
- Ⓒ 14 students
- Ⓓ 2 students

2.

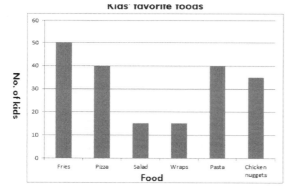

The third graders in Valley Elementary School were asked to pick their favorite food from 6 choices. The results are shown in the bar graph. Which food was the favorite of the most children?

- Ⓐ Pizza
- Ⓑ Pasta
- Ⓒ Fries
- Ⓓ Salad

3.

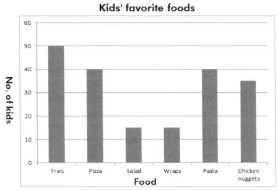

Kids' favorite foods

The third graders in Valley Elementary School were asked to pick their favorite food from 6 choices. The results are shown in the bar graph.

What are the 2 foods that kids like the least?

Ⓐ Fries and Pizza
Ⓑ Pizza and Pasta
Ⓒ Pasta and Chicken Nuggets
Ⓓ Salad and Wraps

4. Find the total number of each coin. Use the tally chart to draw a bar graph.

Coins in John's Piggy Bank		
Coin	**Tally**	**Number of Coins**
Penny	ⅢⅢ ⅢⅢ ⅢⅢ ⅢⅢ ‖	
Nickel	ⅢⅢ ⅢⅢ ⅢⅢ ‖‖	
Dime	ⅢⅢ ⅢⅢ ‖‖‖	
Quarter	ⅢⅢ ⅢⅢ ⅢⅢ ‖	

5. Which of the following answer choices completes the analogy?

Clear is to sunny
as gloomy is to _____

Ⓐ fair
Ⓑ shiny
Ⓒ cloudy
Ⓓ unclouded

6. Which of the following answer choices could replace the underlined words without changing the meaning of the sentence?

The spaghetti was <u>rich with flavor</u>.

Ⓐ tasty
Ⓑ bland
Ⓒ vanilla
Ⓓ nasty

7. Which of the following answer choices could replace the underlined words without changing the meaning of the sentence? Circle the correct answer choice from the options given.

Derrick is <u>very funny</u>.

Ⓐ serious
Ⓑ boring
Ⓒ somber
Ⓓ hilarious

8. Which of the following answer choices means the opposite of the underlined word in the sentence below?

The look on Ms. Morris' face after the test results were in was almost <u>a snarl</u>.

Ⓐ glare
Ⓑ scowl
Ⓒ smile
Ⓓ grimace

Challenge Yourself!

- **Graphs**
- **Shades of Word Meanings**

http://www.lumoslearning.com/a/dc3-44

Day 4

See Page 7 for Signup details

Day 5

1. **What unit should you use to measure the length of a book?**

   Ⓐ Kilometers
   Ⓑ Meters
   Ⓒ Centimeters
   Ⓓ Grams

2. **About how long is a new pencil?**

   Ⓐ 8 inches
   Ⓑ 8 feet
   Ⓒ 8 yards
   Ⓓ 8 miles

3. **Which of these is the best estimate for the length of a football?**

   Ⓐ 1 foot
   Ⓑ 2 feet
   Ⓒ 6 feet
   Ⓓ 4 feet

4. **Fill in the correct answer in the blanks shown in the table.**

Measurement in inches	Measurement in half inches	Measurement in quarter inches
$3\frac{1}{2}$ inches	7 half inches	14 quarter inches
$2\frac{1}{2}$ inches		
	11 half inches	
		26 quarter inches

5. Which of the following sentences has the same meaning as the sentence below?
The principal was infuriated that someone had pulled the fire alarm.

Ⓐ The principal was calm when someone pulled the fire alarm.
Ⓑ The principal was relaxed when someone pulled the fire alarm.
Ⓒ The principal was enraged that someone had pulled the fire alarm.
Ⓓ The principal was excited that someone had pulled the fire alarm.

6. Read the below list of words:
   A. Enormous
   B. Slight
   C. Minute
   D. Average

There were a <u>tremendous</u> number of people at the concert last night.

Which word is similar to the underlined word in above sentence? Write the correct answer in the box given below.

7. Which word is most extreme in its meaning?

Ⓐ cheerful
Ⓑ happy
Ⓒ delighted
Ⓓ overjoyed

8. Which of the following answer choices is least like the word "naughty"?

Ⓐ rowdy
Ⓑ behaved
Ⓒ evil
Ⓓ unruly

Challenge Yourself!

- **Measuring Length**
- **Connecting Related Words**

http://www.lumoslearning.com/a/dc3-45

Day 5

See Page 7 for Signup details

1.

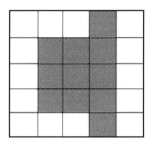

=1 Square Unit

What is the area of the shaded region?

Ⓐ 10 square units
Ⓑ 8 square units
Ⓒ 11 square units
Ⓓ 15 square units

2. Find the area of this figure.

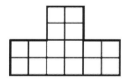

=1 Square Unit

Ⓐ 22 square units
Ⓑ 20 square units
Ⓒ 18 square units
Ⓓ 16 square units

3. Find the area of this figure.

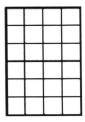

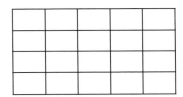

(A) 22 square units
(B) 20 square units
(C) 24 square units
(D) 28 square units

4. Which of the following are possible ways to find the area of this figure? Each box is 1 square unit. Select all correct answers.

(A) Count the total number of square units
(B) Multiplying the length by the width of the figure
(C) Multiplying the number of square units by 2
(D) Subtracting the length of the figure from the width

5. Which of the following domain specific words means "the number below the line in a fraction and tells how many equal parts there are in the whole"? Circle the correct answer choice

    Ⓐ fragment
    Ⓑ denominator
    Ⓒ reproduction
    Ⓓ difference

6. In which class would you most likely talk about "mammals"?

    Ⓐ Math
    Ⓑ Social Studies
    Ⓒ English Language Arts
    Ⓓ Science

7. If your teacher asked you to list a "sequence of events" from a story that you just read, what is she asking you to do?

    Ⓐ The teacher wants you to put the events in order as the occurred in the story.
    Ⓑ The teacher wants you to summarize the story in your own words.
    Ⓒ The teacher wants you to list the main idea and the supporting points from the story.
    Ⓓ The teacher wants you to write your own story that has a similar plot as the story you read.

8. If your teacher wants you to "justify" your answer, what is your teacher asking you to do?

This Week's Online Activities

- Reading Assignment
- Vocabulary Practice
- Write Your Summer Diary

https://www.lumoslearning.com/a/slh3-4

See Page 7 for Signup details

Weekly Fun Summer Photo Contest

Take a picture of your summer fun activity and share it on Twitter or Instagram

Use the **#SummerLearning** mention

@LumosLearning on Twitter or

@lumos.learning on Instagram

Tag friends and increase your chances of winning the contest

Participate and stand a chance to WIN $50 Amazon gift card!

Lumos Short Story Competition 2022

Write a short story based on your summer experiences and get a chance to win $100 cash prize + 1 year free subscription to Lumos StepUp + trophy with a certificate.
To enter the competition follow the instructions.

Step 1

Visit **www.lumoslearning.com/a/tg3-4**
and register for online fun summer program.

Step 2

After registration, your child can upload their summer story by logging into the student portal and clicking on **Lumos Short Story Competition 2022.**

Note: *If you have already registered this book and using online resources need not register again. Students can simply log in to the student portal and submit their story for the competition.*
Visit: www.lumoslearning.com/a/slh2022 for more information

Last date for submission is August 31, 2022

Use the space provided below for scratch work before uploading your summer story Scratch Work

2021 Winning Story

In March 2020, I found out that my 7th-grade exams were canceled. At first, I was excited, but I soon realized that these changes would upend my expectations for school. Over time, my classmates and I realized that the global coronavirus pandemic was not something to be excited about and would have long-lasting effects on our education. My school canceled exams again this year, and, strangely, I found myself missing them. The virus has revealed global inequality regarding health.

Even as America fights the virus, so is it also fighting racism and injustice. The Black Lives Matter movement has shown me how brutal racism can be. The deaths of George Floyd and Breonna Taylor, two African Americans killed by police for no reason, have made me aware of the dangerous injustice in America. Hatred and violence against Asian immigrants are also on the rise. People of color in the US are routinely subjected to prejudice, if not also violence, at the hands of white people. Chinese people are blamed for the "China virus,"; which has led to Asian Americans being attacked. Enduring forms of racism are preventing progress around the world. Racism in society takes many forms, including prejudice, discrimination, and microaggressions. If racism is systemic in America, there will never be true peace or equality until it is uprooted. People see me as a person of color and assume that I'm from Africa because of the color of my skin, even though I am half Black and half white. I don't seem to earn as much respect as a white person would because I am thought of as a foreigner, not a true American. It makes me feel unwelcome and unwanted. I am lucky to have access to technology to keep me engaged in learning. There are still others who don't have the ability to continue learning, whose educational institutions have been shut down by the virus. I have learned that so many people lack access to basic necessities and that racism in America continues to lead to violence and injustice. I aspire to work toward a system that addresses these inequalities in the future. This summer I reflected back on all these things and have learned that no matter what, we all should continue to push on, even through hardships and obstacles.

Submit Your Story Online & WIN Prizes!!!

Student Name: Lillian Olson
Grade: 4

2020 Winning Story

Finding Fun during a Pandemic

This was a weird summer. We did not travel because of COVID-19 and stayed mostly at home and outside around our house. Even when I saw my friends, it was unusual. This summer, I worked and made money helping my parents.

The pandemic allowed me to spend more time inside and I learned many new skills. We made face masks and had to figure out which pattern fits us the best. My sister and I enjoyed creating other arts and crafts projects. Additionally, I have been learning to play instruments such as the piano, guitar, and trombone. We also baked and cooked because we did not go out to eat (at all!). I love baking desserts. The brownies and cookies we made were amazing! I also read for one hour a day and did a workbook by Lumos Learning. I especially loved Math.

Our time outdoors was different this summer. We ordered hens. My family spent a lot of time fixing the coop and setting it up for our 18 chickens. We had a daily responsibility to take care of our chickens in the morning, giving them food and water and in the evening, securing them in their coop. We were surprised that 3 of the hens were actually roosters! Additionally, we exhausted many days gardening and building a retaining wall. Our garden has many different fruits and vegetables. The retaining wall required many heavy bricks, shoveling rocks, and moving dirt around. To cool off from doing all this hard work, we jumped in a stream and went tubing. Our dog, Coco liked to join us.

COVID-19 has also caused me to interact differently with my friends. We used FaceTime, Zoom, and Messenger Kids to chat and video talk with each other. Video chatting is not as fun as being in person with my friends. I love Messenger Kids because it is fun and you can play interactive games with each other.

I had to spend some of my time working. I helped clean my parents' Airbnb. This was busier because of COVID-19. My sister and I will start to sell the chicken eggs once they start to lay which we expect to happen anytime. We had a small business two years ago doing this same thing.

Summer 2020 has been unusual in many ways. We played indoors and outdoors at our house and nearby with family. I have learned new skills and learned to use technology in different ways. Summer of 2020 will never be forgotten!

Submit Your Story Online & WIN Prizes!!!

Answer Key &
Detailed Explanations

Question No.	Answer	Detailed Explanation
1	D	The picture depicts 3 sets of 9 objects which is equivalent to $3 \times 9 = 27$.
2	C	The picture depicts 4 sets of 5 objects which is equivalent to 4×5.
3	D	The picture depicts 4 sets of 7 objects which is equivalent to $4 \times 7 = 28$.

4						
	Number of lions	5	6	9	**8**	**4**
	Total number of legs	20	**24**	**36**	32	16

5	C	Margaret is Amy's mother. The story's opening two lines, "Margaret was a simple lady who lived with her husband Robert. They had a daughter named Amy," explains the relationship between Margaret and Amy. Since Margaret is a lady and her daughter is Amy that makes Margaret her mother.
6	D	Rebecca is the one who slipped on the narrow bridge as she was crossing it. The beginning of paragraph 4 provides this answer for the reader.
7	C	Robert and Margaret went along with the girls because both destinations were across the river. The girls were going to school and Robert and Margaret were going to buy groceries
8	C	Tess' parents were worried because Andrew was sick and they did not have the money needed for his treatment. This answer is found in the opening paragraph of this selection.

Day 2

Question No.	Answer	Detailed Explanation
1	D	There are 100 items that need to be divided into 10 groups. $100 \div 10 = 10$.
2	C	There are 15 items that need to be divided into 3 groups. $15 \div 3 = 5$.
3	A	There are 50 items that need to be divided into 5 groups. $50 \div 5 = 10$.

Question 4

	<	>	=
$30 \div 5$ ____ $42 \div 6$	○	○	●
$72 \div 8$ ____ $63 \div 7$	○	●	○
$54 \div 6$ ____ $56 \div 7$			

Question No.	Answer	Detailed Explanation
5	B	A baby elephant trumpeted loudly. This loud sound woke the monkey. This exact answer is found in the text.
6	A	The swans laughed at the elephant because they thought he was ugly due to his odd appearance. The description the swans use, "long nose, ears like fans, and big wrinkly skin," can cause the reader to draw this conclusion. The elephant also responds by saying, "Why am I so ugly?"
7	C	The bear was frightened of the herd of elephants is the reason that the bear ran away. The author writes, "A herd of wrinkled elephants came charging up. Seeing the herd the frightened bear ran away." The word frightened is used in the text to describe the bear.
8		Students are to illustrate, visualize their thoughts on this poem. Accept all reasonable drawings that depict the poem.

Question No.	Answer	Detailed Explanation
1	B	Product refers to the result of the multiplication of two or more numbers. 54 and 3 are both factors.
2	D	The phrase "twice as many" indicates that if a number is multiplied by 2, the product will reflect two times, or twice, the original amount. In this case, the product of 30 popcorn balls is already known. The product must be then divided by 2 in order to find the amount of cotton candy. $30 \div 2 = 15$.
3	C	The phrase "8 times as many" indicates that if Sue's amount of DVDs is multiplied by 8, the product will be equal to the amount of Monica's DVDs. To solve for Sue use the equation $n \times 8 = 56$. When trying to solve for a missing number in a multiplication equation, you must divide the product by the given number. $56 \div 8 = 7$
4	8	This is a problem on division. Number of cupcakes each boy gets = Total number of cupcakes ÷ number of boys = $48 \div 6 = 8$ cupcakes
5	B	The only saying that matches the actions of the thirsty crow is, "where there's a will, there's a way." The crow wanted the drink so he came up with a way in which to get to the water that at first was unreachable.
6	D	The message taught in this story is that miracles can happen when one has faith. The other three choices don't support a lesson. They are just mere thoughts. Tess, one of the main characters in the story, believed that her money could buy the miracle that her father spoke of. She acts on her faith and goes to buy the miracle.
7	D	Answer D, "persistence is more likely to get you what you want rather than doing nothing at all," is the best answer for the moral of this story. Tess explains her situation to the neurosurgeon after deciding she can buy the miracle. The other choices are not morals. Tess being eight years old is just a fact. The other two choices do not explain anything about what happens in the story.
8	A	The poem clearly states they are building ships using things they find and that one friend got hurt. A is the correct answer. B and C are not correct as it is not ships everywhere and they are not in the actual sea but on stairs.

Question No.	Answer	Detailed Explanation
1	C	To solve for an unknown in a multiplication problem, you must do the opposite operation, which is to divide. You must divide the product by the given factor. 30 ÷ 6=5. n = 5.
2	A	To solve for an unknown in a multiplication problem, you must do the opposite operation, which is to divide. You must divide the product by the given factor. 21 ÷ 7=3. The missing value is 3.
3	A	To solve for an unknown in a multiplication problem, you must do the opposite operation, which is to divide. You must divide the product by the given factor. 36 ÷ 4= 9. The missing value is 9.

4			

Equation	n=7	n=6
$3 \times 8 = 4 \times n$	○	●
$72 \div 9 = 56 \div n$	●	○

Question No.	Answer	Detailed Explanation
5 Part A	C	Amy ignored her fear and jumped into the river because saving her friends was more important than being afraid. This answer is found in paragraph 4.
5 Part B	A	The answer to this question is located in paragraph 5. Robert jumped into the river to save the girls who had fallen or jumped in.
6	A	The action above that demonstrated the elephant was happy was that he danced. This is found in the text in paragraph 3. The author describes the elephant dancing happily.
7	B	The best answer choice for this question is that the little elephant wanted to be like the other elephants because he admired them for being strong. He saw how the other elephants frightened away the bear.
8	C	Based on the story, you can determine that Maggie's problem is how to get everything done that she needs and wants to do.

Week 1

Day 5

Question No.	Answer	Detailed Explanation
1	D	In order for the statement to be true, the answer on both sides of the equal sign must be the same. All of the answer choices are equal except for the last choice. 12 x 1 = 12 and 12 x 12 = 144. 12 x 1 is not equal to 12 x 12.
2	A	Option A is the only one that is true because 11 x 6 = 66 and 6 x 11 = 66. This is an example of the Commutative Property of Multiplication.
3	C	In multiplication, the only time that the number 0 will be the product is when at least one of the factors is 0. Option C is the only choice that fits this rule.

	3 x (5 x 7) = (3 x 5) x 7	3 x 1 = 3	3 x 5 = 5 x 3	3 x (5 + 7) = (3 x 5) + (3 x 7)
Commutative Property			●	
Associative Property	●			
Identity Property		●		
Distributive Property				●

Question No. 4

Question No.	Answer	Detailed Explanation
5	B	"When the little elephant saw the bear he was frightened and trumpeted loudly." This line from the text shows how the event of the bear coming caused the elephant to trumpet loudly. Therefore the best answer choice is B.
6	C	Answer choice C is correct. "The girls fell into the river," can be found in the text to support what happened after Rebecca grabbed Ingrid on the bridge.
7	B	The correct order of this selection should be choice B because it gives the events in the order they happened
8	B	Chart shows some improvement in taking responsibilities.

Question No.	Answer	Detailed Explanation
1	B	5 x 6 = 30 is equivalent to 30 ÷ 6 = 5 because 5 groups of 6 objects is equivalent to 30.
2	C	7 x 3 = 21 is equivalent to 21 ÷ 3 = 7 because 7 groups of 3 objects is equivalent to 21.
3	B	8 x 9 = 72 is equivalent to 72 ÷ 9 = 8 because 8 groups of 9 objects is equivalent to 72.
4 Part a	>	40 ÷ 5 > 54 ÷ 9
4 Part B	<	35 ÷ 7 < 28 ÷ 4
4 Part C	=	18 ÷ 6 = 24 ÷ 8
5	C	"Can't go on" means one cannot continue. This phrase refers to when a person or thing can no longer continue doing something. This answer choice is C.
6	A	Answer choice A is the best meaning for the phrase, "we fell out." This means the siblings had a disagreement. The context clue of a quarrel helps the reader determine the meaning of this phrase.
7	D	Answer choice D is the correct meaning for "charging up." It means rushed forward to attack. This can be determined by the use of words such as crashing and stamping. These actions would happen when something is moving forward quickly.

8		Definition	Vocabulary
		NASA	C. government agency in charge of space exploration
		Launch vehicle	G. powerful rocket used to launch space craft or satellite
		Aeronautics	B. the science of space craft operation
		Astronaut	H. a person who operates spacecraft or works in space, from US
		Space shuttle	F. a reusable space craft, takes off like a rocket, lands like a plane
		Orbit	I. path of a spacecraft or heavenly body as it goes around a planet
		Johnson Space Center	A. headquarters of US manned spacecraft projects and location of Mission Control
		Kennedy Space Center	D. launch facility in Cape Canaveral, FL
		Space Station	E. orbiting space craft designed for occupancy for long period of time

Question No.	Answer	Detailed Explanation
1	C	In multiplication, if one of the factors is 0, the product is also 0.
2	C	The Identity Property of Multiplication states that any number multiplied by 1 equals itself, number so $1 \times 10 = 10$.
3	A	3×8 represents 3 groups of 8 items. There are 24 items in total.

5	x	8	=	40
8	÷	1	=	8
0	÷	7	=	0
6	x	5	=	30

Question No.	Answer	Detailed Explanation
5	A	The correct answer is choice A because the parts of poem are often referred to as stanzas. These parts are not sentences, so they cannot be paragraphs or passages.
6	A	The first answer choice, A, is the line from the story that tells where the astronomer lived, the suburbs. Choices B and C are events from the story but not settings.
7	C	The bold parts of this selection are called headings. These headings tell the reader what the paragraph following them is about.
8	B	Answer choice B is correct. These are the rhyming patterns in the poem. Other answers are not showing rhyming patterns.

Question No.	Answer	Detailed Explanation
1	C	First, calculate how many cards Danny has by subtracting 11 from 47; 47 - 11 = 36. Then divide this number by 3 to see how many each classmate will receive; 36 ÷ 3 = 12.
2	C	First, calculate how many students are in each class. The first class has 3 rows of 7 students and 3 x 7 = 21. The second class has 4 rows of 5 students and 4 x 5 = 20. Then add both totals to calculate the total number of students outside; 21 + 20 = 41.
3	D	First, calculate how much more money Jessica needs to save by subtracting what she has from what she needs; $100 - $60 = $40. Jessica needs 40 more dollars. Now divide 40 dollars by the amount she makes each hour of babysitting to find how many more hours she needs to work to earn the rest of the money; $40 ÷ 10 = 4.
4	D	First step is total number of bottles the farmer needed: 22 ÷ 2 = 11. Next step: Number of bottles left after he spilled 6 bottles: 11 - 6 = 5. So, Option (D) is to be circled.
5	C	"I" is the narrator of the poem. The pronoun I is used throughout the poem. The other choices are images in the poem that are referred to by name.
6	C	A narrator is telling the story. The reader knows this because Pearl's name is used, not "I." This means Pearl did not tell the story. A bus driver and Pearl's mother are not mentioned in the story.

7		Yes	No
	The man	○	●
	The goose	○	●
	A narrator, outside of the story	●	○
	The golden eggs	○	●

You can tell it is someone telling the story, the narrator or someone outside of the story. The other options are characters in the story.

8	Some ideas may include on the positive side that no weapons would come to school, and that the school hallways would be safer and have order to them.
	For negative effects it might include that the cost to parents is too high or that students' privacy would be violated.
	Solutions could include finding out what other schools are doing, having an assembly to go over reasons why the school decided to change the rules, allowing special needs or small frame students to bring carts, or to try a week without backpacks and carts vs a week with backpacks and carts.

Question No.	Answer	Detailed Explanation
1	C	An even number is any number whose ones digit is one of the following numbers: 0, 2, 4, 6, 8. Option C is the only choice that fits this criteria.
2	C	An odd number is any number whose ones digit is one of the following numbers: 1, 3, 5, 7, 9. Option C is the only choice that does not contain any numbers that fit this criteria.
3	C	The rule states that when two even numbers are added, the answer will always be even. For example, 34 + 12 = 46.

	2	4	5	7
A number has a four in its ones place. The number can be a multiple of _____.	●	●	○	●
A number has a five in its ones place. The number can be a multiple of _____.	○	○	●	●
A number has a zero in its ones place. The number can be a multiple of _____.	●	●	●	●
A number has a three in its ones place. The number can be a multiple of _____.	○	○	○	●

4

Statement 1: A multiple of 5 cannot have four in the ones place. A multiple of 2 or 4 or 7 can have four in the ones place. For ex. 2 x 2 = 4, 4 x 6 = 24, 2 x 7 = 14.
Statement 2: A multiple of 2 or 4 cannot have five in the ones place. A multiple of 5 or 7 can have five in the ones place. For ex. 5 x 7 = 35.
Statement 3: Any number when multiplied by 10 results in a number with a zero in the ones place. For ex. 2 x 10 = 20, 4 x 10 = 40, 5 x 10 = 50, 7 x 10 = 70.
Statement 4: Multiples of 2, or 4, or 5 cannot have three in the ones place. A multiple of 7 can have 3 in the ones place. For ex. 7 x 9 = 63.

Question No.	Answer	Detailed Explanation
5	C	Pizza is the most popular item on the lunch menu at Curbside School. This can be determined because pizza has the tallest bar graph.
6	D	Numbers, answer choice D is the correct answer. Numbers would allow the reader to see the exact number of students who like the different foods. This would help to determine which food is liked almost as much as spaghetti.
7	A	Hamburgers is the correct answer to what food item is the second favorite. This is represented by the bar graph because hamburgers have the second highest bar

	Monday	Tuesday	Wednes-day	Thurs-day	Friday	Saturday	Sunday	**Totals**
Playing Video Games	4 hours	4 hours	3 hours	3 hours	2 hours	3 hours	3 hours	**22 hours**
Doing Home-work	30 min	30 min	1 hour	1 hour	1 hour	none	none	**4 hours**
Doing Chores	15 min	15 min	45 min	45 min	45 min	2 hours	1 hour	**5 hours 45 min**
Going to Bed On Time	Not done	Not done	Not done	Done	Not done	Done	Done	**Went to be on time 3 days**

8

Students must add up the time for each activity, then add the number of days that he did go to bed on time.

Question No.	Answer	Detailed Explanation
1	D	Moving from right to left, the positions are as follows: ones, tens, hundreds, thousands, ten thousands. 9 - 10's is the same as 9 x 10 = 90.
2	A	Moving from right to left, the positions are as follows: ones, tens, hundreds, thousands, ten thousands.
3	C	Moving from right to left, the positions are as follows: ones, tens, hundreds, thousands, ten thousands.

4		

Number	Number when rounded to the nearest ten	Number when rounded to the nearest hundred
2,349	2,350	2,300
4,092	**4,090**	**4,100**
8,396	**8,400**	**8,400**

Question No.	Answer	Detailed Explanation
5	B	"He looks different than the other animals" is correct. Throughout the opening of the text, the author gives a physical description of the elephant.
6	A	A is correct. When the little elephant expressed wanting to be like the big elephants they told him he was.
7	D	According to the last part of the text, the neighbor questions the astronomer as to why he is not seeing things on earth, but paying attention to things in heaven. Therefore, choice D is the best answer.
8	B	The articles do not show answer A. Answer B does note the similarities between China and India. Answer C does not, nor does D. Answer B is the only correct answer.

Question No.	Answer	Detailed Explanation
1	B	When these numbers are lined up correctly and then added, the results are:

$$\begin{array}{r} 70000 \\ 6000 \\ 800 \\ 60 \\ + \quad 2 \\ \hline 76,862 \end{array}$$

Question No.	Answer	Detailed Explanation
2	C	Difference refers to the answer when two numbers are subtracted. Option C is the only choice where the difference will be 29.
3	C	In order to solve for the unknown number in an addition problem, subtract the two known numbers. 756 - 356 = 400.

	Hundreds	Tens	Ones
	2	1	5
+	6	3	4
Total	8	4	9

4 — The correct numbers are 6 (hundreds), 1 (tens), and 4 (ones). When adding three-digit numbers, start by adding the numbers in the ones place. Then add the numbers in the tens place. The last step is to add the numbers in the hundreds place. 215 + 634= 849.

Question No.	Answer	Detailed Explanation
5	at the end of the forest	Brandon lives at the end of the forest. This answer is located in the opening sentence of the story.
6	A	The first answer choice is correct. Brandon finds his courage in the setting of the forest. This line is found near the end of the reading selection. "He crossed the forest confidently with courage."
7	C	Answer choice three is the best answer for this question. The likely setting of this story is a forest since the author explains that Brandon and his mother live on the end of a forest and later that Brandon gets his confidence and courage as he travels through the forest.
8	D	Answer choice D is the correct answer. The author describes Jasmine leaving the car, looking at the old farmhouse, and that her G scooped her up and told her to come on into her home. This allows the reader to know that Jasmine traveled somewhere other than her home or her daddy's home. There is no mention of a friend in the story.

Day 2

Question No.	Answer	Detailed Explanation
1	B	6 x 10 is equivalent to 6 sets of 10 which equals a total of 60.
2	C	Product refers to the answer when numbers are multiplied. 10 x 10 is equivalent to 10 sets of 10 which equals a total of 100.
3	C	5 x 40 is equivalent to 5 x 4 tens which equals a total of 200.

	630	320	540	450
9 x 60 =			●	
4 x 80 =		●		
90 x 5 =				●
90 x 7 =	●			

4

When we are multiplying a number by another number which is a multiple of ten, multiply the first number with the non-zero part of the second number. Then add one zero to the product obtained at the end.

In the first problem, we are multiplying 9 by 60. 9 x 6 = 54. Now add one zero at the end to get the product of 9 x 60; 9 x 60 = 540.

In the second problem, we are multiplying 4 by 80. 4 x 8 = 32. Now add one zero at the end to get the product of 4 x 80; 4 x 80 = 320.

In the third problem, we are multiplying 5 by 90 (note that 90 x 5 = 5 x 90; commutative property). 5 x 9 = 45. Now add one zero at the end to get the product of 5 x 90; 5 x 90 = 450.

In the fourth problem, we are multiplying 7 by 90 (note that 90 x 7 = 7 x 90; commutative property). 7 x 9 = 63. Now add one zero at the end to get the product of 7 x 90; 7 x 90 = 630.

Question No.	Answer	Detailed Explanation
5	C	The passage explicitly states that Robert Johnson was a Blues Musician from the Mississippi Delta. The passage does not mention Chicago or that Robert Johnson was from Africa. The 2nd paragraph is all about Robert Johnson.
6	B	The passage tells the reader that the Blues began in the Deep South. It mentions an African influence. It does not state that the origin of the Blues was Africa. The passage does not mention Europe or the Northern states of the U.S.
7	B	The passage explicitly describes that the Blues have influenced many types of music, especially Rock and Roll, Rap, and Country.
8	D	He should share with parents, counselor and friend since they were all concerned and wanted him to do better.

Question No.	Answer	Detailed Explanation
1	C	When forming a fraction, the numerator will be the part of the whole and the denominator will be the whole or all parts together. In this case, there are 3 vowels (the part) and there are 7 total letters (the whole). The fraction should be 3/7.
2	B	When forming a fraction, the numerator will be the part of the whole and the denominator will be the whole or all parts together. In this case, there are 2 yellow tiles (the part) and there are 10 total tiles (the whole). The fraction should be 2/10.
3	C	When forming a fraction, the numerator will be the part of the whole and the denominator will be the whole or all parts together. In this case, there is 1 piece (the part) and there are 4 pieces (the whole). The fraction should be 1/4.
4	B&D	The circle is divided into 8 equal parts. 1 of the 8 parts represents $\frac{1}{8}$ of the whole circle. The fraction $\frac{8}{8}$ represents the whole circle. $\frac{8}{8} = 1$.
5	D	Answer choice D "Every thing in nature follows a pattern" is the only answer choice that is a true fact according to the text.
6	B	The answer to this question is B, referencing how bees make patterns. The other choices are not possible according to this text.
7	B	If you selected B, you picked the right answer. Each detail in the passage tells of an area where robots can do something that a person could not do.
8	D	Answers A,B,C can all be summarizations of the passage, but D is not part of the passage nor a summary. D is the best answer to which is Not a summary.

Day 4

Question No.	Answer	Detailed Explanation
1	A	The number line is divided into four segments and the dot is at the first segment of the four. The fraction is 1/4.
2	A	The number line is divided into two segments and the dot is at the first segment of the two. The fraction is 1/2.
3	C	The number line is divided into eight segments and the dot is at the third segment of the eight. The fraction is 3/8.

	4/4	8/9	5/8

4		In the first number line, the interval from 0 to 1 is taken as the whole and is divided into 9 equal segments. Each segment has a size $\frac{1}{9}$. The dot is at the end of the 8th segment from 0. So, it represents $\frac{8}{9}$. In the second number line, the interval from 0 to 1 is taken as the whole and is divided into 8 equal segments. Each segment has a size $\frac{1}{8}$. The dot is at the end of the 5th segment from 0. So, it represents $\frac{5}{8}$. In the third number line, the interval from 0 to 1 is taken as the whole and is divided into 4 equal segments. Each segment has a size $\frac{1}{4}$. The dot is at the end of the 4th segment from 0. So, it represents $\frac{4}{4}$ or 1.
5	A	Before tourists could visit Kentucky for horse racing, there had to be horse racing facilities for tourists. Kentucky is known for the Kentucky Derby which takes place at Churchill Downs. Therefore, "Churchill Downs was built" is the correct answer.
6	B	Answer choice B is correct. Line number 2 of the first paragraph provides this answer. The word "but" signals she did not do as planned, go to college. The reason is included in this paragraph.

Question No.	Answer	Detailed Explanation
5	A	Before tourists could visit Kentucky for horse racing, there had to be horse racing facilities for tourists. Kentucky is known for the Kentucky Derby which takes place at Churchill Downs. Therefore, "Churchill Downs was built" is the correct answer.
6	B	Answer choice B is correct. Line number 2 of the first paragraph provides this answer. The word "but" signals she did not do as planned, go to college. The reason is included in this paragraph.
7	A	Answer choice A is correct. The other three were mentioned in the passage but they were NOT highlighted as being a positive effect.
8		In the context of the passage, the students can imagine and give their response. The passage says that the Romans felt protected by the Alps, so they were not prepared for an attack. The passage also says that the Romans panicked because they had never seen animals like the elephants. If they were unprepared and panicky, it is more likely that Hannibal defeated the Romans than that the Romans defeated.

Question No.	Answer	Detailed Explanation
1	A	If the numerators of two or more fractions are the same, the fraction with the greatest denominator is the smallest fraction. Option A is the only choice that has the numbers lined up from the greatest to the smallest denominator.
2	C	In order for a fraction to be between 1/2 and 1, it would have to be greater than 1/2. Option C is the only choice that fits this criteria. Since 4/8 = 1/2, 5/8 would be greater than 1/2. 3/1 is greater than 1 whole, so that is too large. 1/3 is smaller than 1/2.
3	C	In order for a fraction to be between 0 and 1/2, it would have to be less than $\frac{1}{2}$. Option C is the only choice that fits this criteria.
4	$\frac{6}{10}$	In this problem, we are comparing the fractions with the same numerators. It means the whole (represented by the numerator) in the fractions is the same, and it is divided into different numbers of equal parts (represented by the denominator). Therefore, the fraction with the greater denominator is less than the fraction with the smaller denominator. So, $\frac{6}{10} < \frac{6}{9} < \frac{6}{5} < \frac{6}{4}$.
5	C	Carnivore means meat eating animal, choice C. The reader can determine this by reading the first sentence, animals eat other animals. The next sentence states these animals are carnivores. Therefore, animals eating other animals would be carnivores.
6	C	Answer choice C, water heating up and turning into vapor, is the meaning of evaporation. "They" in the text refers to clouds. Clouds form when lots of vapors get together. Vapor is formed when the sun heats up water sources such as lakes, rivers, and puddles.
7	D	Population refers to the number of people, which is answer choice D. The reader can determine this by reading, "thousands of babies are being born adding to the population." Babies are human and considered part of a group or society of people. This is how an area's population is determined.
8	D	The phrase, "give students access to many resources," helps the reader determine that the meaning of access is connection, answer choice D. Schools often spend money on extra classroom resources, like dictionaries and calculators, to help students learn. If students have the ability to use the resources on a phone instead, they have an additional connection to the resources other than having to use the ones school's buy.

Day 1

Question No.	Answer	Detailed Explanation
1	B	The hour hand (the shorter hand) is past the 2nd hour but has not reached the 3rd hour, and the minute hand (the longer hand) is past 15 minutes but has not yet reached 20 minutes.
2	D	The hour hand (the shorter hand) is past the 5th hour but has not reached the 6th hour, and the minute hand (the longer hand) is past 45 minutes but has not yet reached 50 minutes.
3	C	The hour hand (the shorter hand) is pointing to the 10th hour, and the minute hand (the longer hand) is past 0 minutes but has not yet reached 5 minutes.

4

	9:42	11:58	2:03
(clock 1)		●	
(clock 2)			●
(clock 3)	●		

(1) In the first clock, the hour hand (the shorter hand) has passed the 11th hour but not yet at the 12th hour.
At the start of the hour, the minute hand (the longer hand) points directly to 12, and it takes 5 minutes to move from one number to the next number and one minute to move from one tick to the next tick.
So, the minute hand is at 58 minutes (5 x 11 + 3 = 58).
Therefore, the clock shows 11:58.
(2) In the second clock, the hour hand (the shorter hand) has passed the 2nd hour but not yet at the 3rd hour.
The minute hand is at 3 minutes (1 x 3 = 3).
Therefore, the clock shows 2:03.
(3) In the third clock, the hour hand (the shorter hand) has passed the 9th hour but not yet at the 10th hour.
The minute hand is at 42 minutes (5 x 8 + 2 = 42).
Therefore, the clock shows 9:42.

Question No.	Answer	Detailed Explanation
5	C	This author helps the reader locate information inside the text by numbering the sentences sequentially. Answer choice C is correct.
6	B	The first sentence of number 4 is about the jobs of bees. Answer B is correct.
7	B	This selection is about multiple ways to stay healthy, and answer choice B is correct. The other choices are examples of specific ways to stay healthy.
8	B	In this poem, the author uses apostrophes to break the words into syllables. For example, "yel'low" has the apostrophe between the double consonants which is a rule when dividing syllables of words with double consonants.

Question No.	Answer	Detailed Explanation
1	A	Counting back from 10:02 to 10:00 is 2 minutes. Then, counting back from 10:00 back to 9:12 is an additional 48 minutes, making the total elapsed time 50 minutes.
2	C	Subtract the beginning time from the ending time; 7:35 back to 7:11 is 24 minutes.
3	D	Subtract the time Tanya began walking from the time she arrived home; 3:56 back to 3:31 is 25 minutes.
4	B	We have to subtract the time Tim left home from the time he returned; 3:45 PM - 11:30 AM. From 11:30 AM to 12 noon is 30 minutes of elapsed time. From 12 noon to 3:00 PM is 3 hours of elapsed time. From 3:00 PM to 3:45 PM is 45 minutes of elapsed time. Therefore, total elapsed time = 30 minutes + 3 hours + 45 minutes = 3 hours and 75 minutes. 3 hours and 75 minutes = 4 hours and 15 minutes.
5	B	The paragraph explains that hexagons are six sided figures. This math information is useful when writing about properties of a hexagon, answer choice B.
6	do not pick it up	The text explains that this frog is dangerous even if it is touched.
7	C	Based on the text, a person who enjoys shopping, might not enjoy a trip to Kentucky. Nowhere in the text can the reader find information about shopping. The other three answer choices provided in the text are enjoyable things to do in Kentucky.
8		In lines 1 and 2 of the text, the reader is informed that Patty stays all day without her family and that the nearest house is miles away

Question No.	Answer	Detailed Explanation
1	D	The word "pound" after the number 40 indicates that 40 is a measurement of weight.
2	B	Kilograms are used to measure the mass of large, solid objects such as a table.
3	A	The amount of a liquid is also called its volume. Option C and D are not used to measure volume. Option B would be too large to measure water in a small bowl. Option A is the only logical choice.
4		This is a two-step problem. First, we calculate the total amount of water in the 8 coolers by multiplying the number of coolers (8) by the capacity of each water cooler (7 liters); 8 x 7 = 56 liters. Next, we calculate the amount of water consumed by subtracting the amount of water remained from the total amount of water; 56 - 5 = 51 liters.
5	A	"A" is the correct answer choice because Elizabeth would have to travel south on Vernon in order to reach Mill Street.
6	B	"B" is the correct answer choice because if Elizabeth was walking west on River Street she would travel on River, Hill, Grove, and School Streets in order to reach the school.
7	C	"C" is the correct answer choice because Venus and Mercury take fewer days than Earth to orbit the sun. You can find this information from the passage and the illustration.
8	D	"D" is the correct answer choice because both the passage and the timeline tell you that ice cream was first advertised in the U.S. in 1777.

Day 4

Question No.	Answer	Detailed Explanation
1	B	The chart shows 3 sets of 5 tallies for Mrs. B's class in the "yes" column. Multiplying 3 x 5 the tallies represent 15 kids.
2	C	The number 14 in the "yes" column for Mrs. A's class represents 14 votes.
3	D	The "Total" row displays the overall number of votes. There is a total of 41 votes represented in the "No" column.
4		The left side of the Venn diagram shows the number of people who own only cats. This is 2 people The right side shows the number of people who own only dogs which is 3 people. The center overlapping portion shows the number of people who own both cat and dog which is 2. We need number of people who own only cat / the number of people who own only dogs which is $\frac{2}{3}$.
5	B	The author finds the ostrich extraordinary because he chose to write about it. Answer choice B is correct. Answer choices C and D cannot be correct based on the text.
6	A	Answer choice A is correct. The fourth sentence supplies the reader with this answer.
7	B	According to this text, answer choice B is correct. The other choices are NOT true based on the paragraph.
8	B	By ending the text with a question, the author wants the reader to answer the question for themselves. In order to do that, the reader must think about the information provided first.

Question No.	Answer	Detailed Explanation
1	C	Options A, B, and D are all customary units. Option C is the only metric unit.
2	B	A meter is just slightly longer than a yard. That is why a meterstick and a yardstick are almost the same length. 1 yard = 36 inches. 1 meter $\approx$ 39 inches.
3	C	Decimeters and centimeters are both too small to measure a table. Kilometers are used to measure long distances or lengths. Option C is the most appropriate.

	4	6	8
How many fish are $16\frac{1}{2}$ inches long?	○	○	●
How many more fish are 16 inches long than 17 inches?	●	○	○
How many fish are less than $15\frac{3}{4}$ inches long?	○	●	○

4

X = 2 fish. There are 4 Xs at $16\frac{1}{2}$ inches. Therefore, the number of fish that are $16\frac{1}{2}$ inches long = 2 x 4 = 8

There are 4 Xs at 16 inches. Therefore, there are 8 (2 x 4) fish that are 16 inches long. There are 2 Xs at 17 inches. Therefore, there are 4 (2 x 2) fish which are 17 inches long. Therefore, there are 4 (8 - 4 = 4) more fish which are 16 inches long than 17 inches.

There are 2 (2 x 1) fish which are 15 inches long, and there are 4 (2 x 2) fish which are $15\frac{1}{2}$ inches long. Therefore, the number of fish which are less than $15\frac{3}{4}$ inches = 2 + 4 = 6.

| 5 | D | "D" is the correct answer choice because it is the only one that accurately describes a similarity in the two passages. "Both Cajuns and Creoles have impacted the Louisiana lifestyle." The other three answer choices are not accurate descriptions of a similarity. |

Question No.	Answer	Detailed Explanation
6	A	"A" is the correct answer choice because it is the only one that accurately describes a difference in the two passages. "Cajuns fled Canada because they were not allowed to practice the Catholic religion. Creoles are people who live in New Orleans and are from French or Spanish family roots." The other three answer choices are not accurate descriptions of a difference.
7	C	"C" is the correct answer choice because it is the only one that accurately highlights a key detail from the passages. The others are not key points that are highlighted in both passages.
8	B	This answer choice is correct because in passage 1 Sara is very excited about picture day and in passage 2 Melissa is not excited about picture day. Answer choice A is incorrect because both girls are not excited about picture day at school. Answer choice C is incorrect because both girls did not wear new dresses for picture day. Melissa wore her sister's hand-me-down. Answer choice D is incorrect because neither passage said if the girls went to different schools or the same school, so this information was not provided.

Question No.	Answer	Detailed Explanation
1	C	Area is a 2 dimensional attribute, so it must be represented in square units. Area is a measure of how many identical squares (or parts of identical squares) would be needed to cover a figure.
2	D	A postage stamp is a rectangle measuring about 1 inch on each side. Therefore, the area of a postage stamp is about 1 square inch. The other objects are all too large to measure 1 square inch as this is a very small measurement.
3	A	Area of a rectangle is calculated by multiplying length by width: 12 inches x 20 inches = 240 square inches.
4	B	Area of the square B is one third the area of the rectangle A. It means, we have to divide the area of the rectangle A by 3 to get the area of the square B. Area of the square B = 75 ÷ 3 = 25 sq. cm. Area of a square = side length x side length. Area of the square B = 25 sq. cm. What is the number when multiplied by itself will give 25? It is 5. Therefore, side length = 5 cm.
5	B	If you chose B, you picked the right answer. If a word ends in a consonant followed by a y, change the y to "i" and add "-es."
6	A	If you chose A, you picked the correct spelling. If the word ends in a vowel followed by a y, do not change the y to "i". Just add "-s."
7	Butter-flies	Remember to change the y to "i," and add "-es," if the letter before the y is a consonant, not a vowel.
8	B	Happy is not a person, place, thing, or idea. It is describing a noun. This makes it an adjective.

Question No.	Answer	Detailed Explanation
1	A	Area is calculated by multiplying length by width: 3 feet x 29 feet = 87 square feet. (Note: 3 x 29 = 29 + 29 + 29 = 87)
2	D	Area is calculated by multiplying length by width: 12 yards x 15 yards = 180 square yards. [Note: 15 x 12 = (15 x 10) + (15 x 2) = 150 + 30 = 180]
3	C	Area of a rectangle is calculated by multiplying length by width. To find the area of this rectangle, multiply 63 x 33.
4	C	Area is calculated by multiplying length by width: 2 meters x 4 meters = 8 square meters.
5	B	"Team" refers to the group of players. Charlene is also a proper noun, but is not one of the answer choices.
6	He, her, she, and it	He, her, she and it are the pronouns that replace the nouns Alice, Jim, and gift.
7	B	We need a pronoun to replace Monica. The correct choice is "her".
8	A	"We", "us" and "She and I" are all second person pronouns. Since the flowers were brought to "me", the speaker would not use a second person pronoun. The best pronoun to complete this sentence is "they".

Question No.	Answer	Detailed Explanation
1	C	The perimeter of a shape is the distance around the shape.
2	B	A plane figure is a two-dimensional (flat) shape. Area and perimeter are both associated with these types of objects. Volume and weight apply to 3-dimensional figures.
3	A	To find the perimeter of a rectangle, total the lengths of its four sides. 4 + 1 + 4 + 1 = 10 units

	15 sq. cm.	10 sq. cm.	12 sq. cm.
Perimeter = 16 cm	✓		✓
Perimeter = 14 cm		✓	✓
Perimeter = 22 cm		✓	

4

Let L be the length of the rectangle and W be the width of the rectangle. Perimeter = 2 (L + W)

(1) Perimeter = 16; 2 x (L + W) = 16; L + W = 16 ÷ 2 = 8. We have to find the length and the width of the rectangle whose sum is 8 cm, and then find the area. Find the areas of the rectangles by substituting L = 1, 2, 3 etc. Among the choices given, there are 2 possible areas. (a) If L = 2, W = 8 - 2 = 6 . Area = L x W = 2 x 6 = 12 sq. cm. (b) If L = 3, W = 8 - 3 = 5. Area = 3 x 5 = 15 sq. cm.

(2) Perimeter = 14; 2 x (L + W) = 14; L + W = 14 ÷ 2 = 7. We have to find the length and the width of the rectangle whose sum is 7 cm, and then find the area. Find the areas of the rectangles by substituting L = 1, 2, 3 etc. Among the choices given, there are 2 possible areas. (a) If L = 2, W = 7 - 2 = 5. Area = 2 x 5 = 10 sq. cm. (b) If L = 3, W = 7 - 3 = 4. Area = 3 x 4 = 12 sq. cm.

(3) Perimeter = 22; 2 x (L + W) = 22; L + W = 22 ÷ 2 = 11. We have to find the length and the width of the rectangle whose sum is 11 cm, and then find the area. Find the areas of the rectangles by substituting L = 1, 2, 3 etc. Among the choices given, there is only one possibility. If L = 1, W = 11 - 1 = 10. Area = 1 x 10 = 10 sq. cm.

Question No.	Answer	Detailed Explanation
5	B	This answer choice B is correct because the plural form of "mouse" is mice. Answer choice A is incorrect because children is the correct plural form not childrens. Answer C is incorrect because "doctors" is the correct plural form and doctores is not. Answer D is incorrect because "women" is the correct plural form and womans is not.
6	D	This answer choice is correct because "deer" is the only answer choice that is used as a plural noun in the sentence. "We" is a pronoun so it is not the correct answer.
7	B	This is the correct answer because "berries" is the correct plural form of the word "berry."
8	C	This is the only answer choice that incorrectly changes a plural noun to its singular form. Wifes=Wife

Day 4

Question No.	Answer	Detailed Explanation
1	C	By definition, a polygon is a plane (flat), closed figure with only straight sides.
2	C	A polygon must have only straight sides. A circle is the only option that does not fit this criteria. Since it is curved.
3	A	A rectangle is a quadrilateral (4-sided polygon) with 4 right angles.
4	C & D	The first figure is a trapezoid. It has one pair of parallel sides. The second figure is a pentagon. It has no parallel sides. The third figure is a regular hexagon. It has 3 sets of parallel sides. The fourth figure has one set of parallel sides.
5	C	This is the correct answer choice because the word crime is the only example of an abstract noun.
6	A	This answer choice listed as "beauty" is the only abstract noun.
7	B	The correct answer is "wisdom" because it is the answer choice that is an abstract noun. The other answer choices give examples of concrete nouns a noun that can be seen, touched, smelled, or heard.
8	Motiva-tion	"Motivation" is the only abstract noun given that is found in the sentence.

Question No.	Answer	Detailed Explanation
1	B	A line of symmetry is an imaginary line that divides an object into two mirror images.
2	B	A line of symmetry is an imaginary line that divides an object into two mirror images. A square can be divided across the length, across the width, down diagonally from left to right, and down diagonally from right to left.
3	C	A line of symmetry is an imaginary line that divides an object into two mirror images. Option C cannot be divided in such a way.
4	B,C,&D	The circle is divided into 8 equal parts. This means that each part has the same area. Divide the total area by 8 to calculate the area of each part; $96 \div 8 = 12$ sq. cm. Each part has an area of 12 sq. cm. (1) When we shade 3 parts, the shaded portion has an area of 3 x 12 = 36 sq. cm. Therefore, option (A) is wrong. (2) When we shade 4 parts, the shaded portion has an area of 4 x 12 = 48 sq. cm. Therefore, option (B) is correct. (3) When we shade 7 parts, the shaded portion has an area of 7 x 12 = 84 sq. cm. Therefore, option (C) is correct. (4) When we shade 2 parts, the shaded portion has an area of 2 x 12 = 24 sq. cm. Therefore, option (D) is correct.
5	C	"Angrily" is an adverb to explain how the verb was acting. We need a verb to complete the sentence. Since the sentence is currently occurring, "growling" is correct.
6	D	If you read through the choices, only one is grammatically correct. "Sleeping" is the correct verb choice. "The monkey was sleeping on the branch of the tree" is the complete sentence.
7	B	"Wander" refers to just walking around without a real plan. "Wonder" refers to think about or ponder. "Yonder" refers to a distant location.
8	B	"I drank three glasses of milk yesterday." "Drank" is the past tense form of the verb drink.

Day 1

1	A	The picture depicts 2 sets of 12 objects which is equivalent to 2 x 12 = 24.
2	A	The picture depicts 4 sets of 4 objects which is equivalent to 4 x 4 = 16.
3	A	The picture depicts 4 sets of 6 objects which is equivalent to 4 x 6 = 24.
4 Part A		Yes, John is correct. 8 x 6 = 8 x (5 + 1). Then John used the distributive property. 8 x (5 + 1) = 8 x 5 + 8 x 1 = 8 x 5 + 8.
4 Part B		Let n be the total number of pens the boys buy all together. n = (number of pens each boy buys) x (number of boys) = 6 x 7 = 42 pens
5	B	This answer choice is correct because it is the past tense form of "play."
6	C	This answer choice correctly labels "will try" as future tense.
7	A	This answer choice is correct because "speaks" is the present tense of the verb.
8	Ride	The question ask for you to change the word "rode" to its present tense. "We ride the merry-go-round at the mall five times." This answer correctly does that because it changes to "ride"

Question No.	Answer	Detailed Explanation
1	D	There are 30 items that need to be sorted into 6 groups. $30 \div 6 = 5$.
2	B	There are 80 items that need to be sorted into groups of 10. $80 \div 10 = 8$.
3	B	There are 15 items that need to be shared with 5 groups. $15 \div 5 = 3$.
4	A & C	The correct answers are A and C. There is a total of 16 stickers to be divided into equal groups. The stickers can be divided into 2 equal groups of 8. The stickers can also be divided into 4 equal groups of 4.
5	C	The subject of the sentence "my sister" is singular, and needs a plural verb. The sentence that is written correctly is "My sister always helps my mother."
6	B	Since "my neighbor and his dog" refers to two subjects, the verb needs to be singular. The sentence that has an agreeing subject and verb is "My neighbor and his dog walk every day."
7	C	The word that completes the sentence properly is "go".
8	will give	Since this sentence is talking about the future, the correct verb phrase to complete it is "will give".

Question No.	Answer	Detailed Explanation
1	A	Marcus' jumping jack is equivalent to 4 times that of Jonathan. $7 \times 4 = 28$.
2	D	Marsha's movie count is equivalent to 3 times that of Jonathan's. $3 \times 4 = 12$.
3	B	There are 4 groups and each group has 9 items. This indicates that if the number of groups is multiplied by the number of items in each group, the product will reflect the total number of items in all. $4 \times 9 = 36$.
4 Part A	x	First, we find the value of $64 \div 8$. $64 \div 8 = 8$. Now, we have to find the correct symbol to make the equation $8 = 2 \underline{\quad} 4$, true. Multiplying 2 by 4, we get 8. Therefore, x (multiplication symbol) is the correct choice.
4 Part B	+	First, we find the value of $42 \div 7$. $42 \div 7 = 6$. Now, we have to find the correct symbol to make the equation $2 \underline{\quad} 4 = 6$, true. If we add 2 and 4, we get 6. Therefore, + (plus) is the correct choice.
5	C	If you look closely at the word "growly", you will notice the root word "growl".
6	B	Since there is nothing being compared here, the best word to complete this sentence is "long". Elongate cannot work because it is missing the necessary ending and would require the form "elongated".
7	B	"Confusing" is the adjective describing the noun, "assignment."
8	mildly	"Disturbed" is the word that is showing action. We then start to look for the word that explains how the disruption occurred. It occurred "mildly", making this the adverb.

Question No.	Answer	Detailed Explanation
1	C	The first step to solve for an unknown in a division problem is to decide which part of the problem is missing: Dividend: n Divisor: 9 Quotient: 8 When solving for the dividend, you must multiply the divisor and the quotient. 9 x 8 = 72. n = 72.
2	B	The first step to solve for an unknown in a division problem is to decide which part of the problem is missing: Dividend: n Divisor: 3 Quotient: 10 When solving for the dividend, you must multiply the divisor and the quotient. 3 x 10 = 30. n = 30.
3	C	The first step to solve for an unknown in a division problem is to decide which part of the problem is missing: Dividend: 45 Divisor: n Quotient: 9 When solving for the divisor, you must divide the dividend by the quotient. 45 ÷ 9 = 5.

		Equation	Product
4	32; 9; 15 and 7	4 x 8=	32
		9	x 7 = 63
		3 x 5=	15
		7	x 1 =7

Question No.	Answer	Detailed Explanation
5	B	This is the correct answer because "rather than" is an example of a subordinating conjunction.
6	D	This is the correct answer because "until" is an example of a subordinating conjunction.
7	A	This answer choice is correct because it accurately defines a coordinating conjunction.
8	But	My mom cooked spaghetti for dinner **but** I really wanted lasagna. The "but" is the only coordinating conjunction used in the given sentence.

Day 5

Question No.	Answer	Detailed Explanation
1	C	In multiplication, the only time that the number 0 will be the product is when at least one of the factors is 0. In division, the only time that the number 0 will be the answer is when the dividend is 0. Option C is the only choice where the equation fits this rule.
2	C	The Identity Property of Multiplication states that any number multiplied by 1 equals itself.
3	A	The Commutative Property of Multiplication states that the order of the factors does not change the answer.
4	A	Associative property is the rule that states that when the grouping of factors changes, the product remains the same. This applies to the equations (2 x 3) x 4 = 24 and 2 x (3 x 4) = 24.
5	B	Clearly, this is providing facts about the giraffe. This is an informative sentence.
6	B	There are two ideas expressed in this sentence. Both are complete. This makes this a compound sentence.
7	C	A complex sentence means that there is one complete idea and a partial idea. Did you notice how the sentence reads: I get a stomach ache? This part of this sentence does not leave the reader with unanswered questions, so it is a complete thought or a simple sentence. When we add the partial idea "When I eat too much candy", the reader is left wondering, "What happens when too much candy is eaten?" This is only part of a sentence, or an incomplete idea. These two combined create a complex sentence.
8	B	Alexander forgot his glasses on the counter, **but** his mom was able to bring them to school for him. "But" is the appropriate conjunction that shows that the situation was okay because the glasses were delivered to school.

Question No.	Answer	Detailed Explanation
1	D	10 x 5 = 50 is equivalent to 50 ÷ 10 = 5 because 10 groups of 5 objects is equivalent to 50.
2	A	4 x 9 = 36 is equivalent to 36 ÷ 4 = 9 because 4 groups of 9 objects is equivalent to 36.
3	C	Since there are 9 students who need 5 sheets each, this is equivalent to 9 x 5 which equals 45, or 45 ÷ 5 = 9.
4	A	Multiplication and division are inverse operations. This means that when two numbers are multiplied, the product we get can be divided by either of the two factors to give the other factor. Here, the product (65) is divided by one of the factors (n) to get the other factor (5). Therefore, the equivalent number sentence is 65 = 5 x n. Note that 5 x n can also be written as n x 5 (commutative property).
5	A	"I" is a proper pronoun. It should always be capitalized, even if it is not at the beginning of the sentence.
6	D	"Mom" is a proper noun. It should always be capitalized unless it has the word "my" in front of it. The correctly written sentence is: I said, "I don't feel well, Mom."
7	A	She said, "Doctor, my child doesn't feel well." This is the correct answer. Given that the person is speaking, the first word inside of the quotation or the dialogue is capitalized. The beginning of the sentence should also be capitalized.

		Correct	Not Correct
8	Little House on the Prairie	✓	
	A Wrinkle in Time	✓	
	The Lion King	✓	
	The Call of the Wild	✓	

Day 2

Question No.	Answer	Detailed Explanation
1	B	5 x 9 represents 5 groups of 9 items. There are 45 items in total.
2	C	Product refers to the answer when numbers are multiplied. 8 x 6 represents 8 groups of 6 items. There are 48 items in total.
3	C	Product refers to the answer when numbers are multiplied. 7 x 7 represents 7 groups of 7 items. There are 49 items in total.
4	C	The quotient refers to the answer when a number is divided by another number. There are 27 items that need to be divided into 9 groups. 27 ÷ 9 = 3.
5	B	The rule in the English language is that if addresses are written on one line, commas must be placed after street address, city,but not after state before zip code. The correct choice is: 1345 Sycamore Street Chicago, IL 123452
6	C	These answers show addresses on one line. The correctly written address is: 8142 Brown Avenue New York, NY 14353
7	A	The questions in the selection show addresses on one line. The correctly written address is: 800 Heartbreak Lane Las Vegas, NV 83902
8		Jamie screamed, "There is a spider!" The punctuation belongs inside or before the closing quotation mark.

Question No.	Answer	Detailed Explanation
1	A	First calculate how many cookies George began with by multiplying 2 and 10; 2 x 10 = 20. Then subtract the number of cookies he gave to his parents from this total; 20 - 12 = 8.
2	A	First calculate the total number of minutes Renae spends doing chores by multiplying 3 and 15; 3 x 15 = 45. Then subtract this number from 60 minutes to see how many minutes she has remaining to do her homework; 60 - 45 = 15.
3	C	First calculate the sale price of the game; $28 - 4 = $24. Then divide this answer by 2 to see how much each girl will pay; $24 ÷ 2 = $12.

4			$50	$5	$10	$4
		Karen had 86 dollars. He bought 7 books. After buying them he had 16 dollars. How much did each book cost?	○	○	●	○
		Jose and his four friends bought a new board game. It was on sale for 20 dollars off. If each of the boys (total 5 of them) paid $6. What was the original cost of the new board game?	●	○	○	○
		A shopkeeper buys 5 pens for $35 and sells them at the rate of $8 per pen. If he sells all the five pens, how much profit he will get?	○	●	○	○
		Jeffrey bought 8 actions figures which cost 3 dollars each from John. John bought 6 books from the amount he received from Jeffrey. If the cost of each book John purchased is the same, what is the cost of each book?	○	○	○	●

Solution to problem 1 : First, subtract $16 from $86 to get the cost of 7 books; 86 - 16 = $70. Then divide $70 by 7 to get the cost of one book. Cost of one book = 70 ÷ 7 = $10.

Solution to problem 2 : First, multiply 5 by $6 to get the total amount paid by the boys; 5 x 6 = $30. Then add $20 to $30 to get the original cost of the new board game; 20 + 30 = $50.

Solution to problem 3 : First, multiply 5 by 8 to calculate the total amount of money the shopkeeper gets; 5 x 8 = $40. Then subtract $35 from $40 to get the profit he earns; 40 - 35 = $5.

Solution to problem 4 : First, multiply 8 by $3 to get the amount received by John; 8 x 3 = $24. Then divide $24 by 6 to get the cost of each book; 24 ÷ 6 = $4.

Question No.	Answer	Detailed Explanation
5	C	This answer choice has a correctly placed comma after "Grant asked." The quotation marks are also correctly placed. Answer choice A is not correct because there are no closing quotation marks after ball and there needs to be a question mark after ball instead of a comma. Answer choice B is not correct because the comma is wrongly placed after Elizabeth and there aren't any open quotation marks in the dialogue. Answer choice D is incorrect because there isn't a comma and the quotation marks are used incorrectly.
6	B	This answer choice is correct because the comma and quotation marks are correctly placed. This answer choice A is incorrect because the quotation marks are around "Amber said." Answer choice C is incorrect because quotation marks surround "He replied,". Answer choice D is incorrect because the whole quote includes suggested Sammie.
7	A	This answer choice is correct because the quotation marks and comma are correctly placed. Answer choice B is incorrect because the quotation does not start with a capital letter, there isn't a comma, and the quotation marks are not properly placed. Answer choice C is incorrect because there aren't any closing quotation marks, and a period is used instead of a comma. Answer choice D is incorrect because the quotation mark is incorrectly placed behind "stated", and a period is used instead of a comma.
8	D	This answer choice D is correct because it was correctly punctuated. Answer choice A is incorrect because there is no comma after papers or closed quotation marks. Also there is no open quotation marks before I.

Question No.	Answer	Detailed Explanation
1	A	The rule states that when two even numbers are multiplied, the product will always be even. For example, 34 x 4 = 136.
2	D	There is not enough information given for us to decide if the number is a multiple of 3, 7, or 9. For example, if the original number was 19, it would not be a multiple of 3, 7, or 9.
3	D	Any multiple of an even number is also even. Numbers that are multiples of 8 are also multiples of 2 and 4 because 2 and 4 are factors of 8.
4	C	When you add two odd numbers, the sum is an even number. Addition and subtraction are inverse operations. Therefore, when you subtract an odd number from an even number, the difference has to be an odd number. If a and b are odd numbers, the sum (c = a + b) is an even number. Therefore, c - a (= b) or c - b (= a) has to be an odd number.
5	C	"Mine" is the only word that sensibly completes this sentence. My things are all mine.
6	D	The correct answer is: Lydia's things are all hers.
7	D	The correct answer is: Billy and Tim's things are theirs.
8	D	Given the incorrect possessives in the other sentences, the correct sentence is: I forgot to invite Julian to my party.

Question No.	Answer	Detailed Explanation
1	C	Moving from right to left, the positions are as follows: ones, tens, hundreds, thousands. In order to round to the nearest hundred, you must look at the number in the tens place. If this number is less than 5, you must round the hundreds number down. If this number is 5 or more, you must round the hundreds number up.
2	A	Moving from right to left, the positions are as follows: ones, tens, hundreds, thousands. In order to round to the nearest hundred, you must look at the number in the tens place. If this number is less than 5, you must round the hundreds number down. If this number is 5 or more, you must round the hundreds number up.
3	B	Moving from right to left, the positions are as follows: ones, tens, hundreds. In order to round to the nearest ten, you must look at the number in the ones place. If this number is less than 5, you must round the tens number down. If this number is 5 or more, you must round the tens number up.
4	500	When rounding to the nearest hundred look at the number in the tens place. If the number is less than 5 round down to the nearest hundred. If the number is 5 or more, round up to the nearest hundred. 489 is nearest to 500 on the number line.
5	B	If you chose B, you picked the right answer. A rule that can help you to remember is that the root word does not change when a suffix or second word is added. When "hiker" is added to "hitch," the result is "hitchhiker." Neither word loses a letter. When the suffix "–ly" is added to "natural," the result is "naturally." Neither the word nor the suffix loses a letter. "Mis-" + "spelled" = "misspelled". Neither the suffix nor the word loses a letter.
6	D	If you chose D, you made the right decision. Words that end in silent –e do not change when the –r ending is added. "Rider" is the correct spelling.
7	D	The misspelled word is thief. The rule, i before e except after c and "eigh," as in "neighbor" and "weigh," doesn't work all of the time. When uncertain, choose "ie" if the sound is "ee."
8	Febuary	"Febuary" is misspelled. This word is missing the "r" following the b. The word should be spelled F-e-b-r-u-a-r-y.

Day 1

Question No.	Answer	Detailed Explanation
1	C	The difference between 94 and 50 is 44. Option C is the only choice where 44 is also the answer.
2	C	In all of the choices, the sum on both sides of the number sentence must be equal. Option C is the only choice where the two sums are not equal. 56+45 = 101 and 54 + 56 = 110.
3	D	The phrase "in all" indicates that the two numbers must be added in order to find the total. 640 + 280 = 920.
4	115	The correct answer is 115. The word 'difference' refers to the subtraction of numbers. When subtracting three-digit numbers, start by subtracting the numbers in the ones place. Then subtract the numbers in the tens place. The last step is to subtract the numbers in the hundreds place. 719 - 604 = 115.
5	C	There are three syllables in the word telescope: tel-e-scope
6	D	There are four syllables in the word astronomer: a-stron-o-mer
7	C	Grad-u-a-tion has four syllable
8	two syllables	Ostrich has two syllables. These syllables are o-strich

Week 8

Question No.	Answer	Detailed Explanation
1	D	6 x 60 is equivalent to 6 x 6 tens which equals a total of 360.
2	D	Product refers to the answer when numbers are multiplied. 70 x 7 is equivalent to 7 tens x 7 which equals a total of 490.
3	A	30 x 7 is equivalent to 3 tens x 7 which equals a total of 210.
4		

a x b =	c
6 x 50 =	300
8 x 60 =	480
70 x 8 =	560
80 x 9 =	720

Question No.	Answer	Detailed Explanation
5	B	Answer choice B is the correct response. Nia must choose a reference source that is based on facts since it is a research paper. The resource must also be about the topic being researched. The other 3 choices have nothing to do with the American Civil War.
6	A	A fiction story about the civil war might give some facts, but Nia might not know for sure which is fiction or which is fact.
7		The answer to this question would be to read an informational book about seashells.
8	B	A synonym for conceal is "wrap," answer choice B. This is found in box number 2 from a thesaurus. The word wrap is used and next to it are synonyms that include the word conceal.

Question No.	Answer	Detailed Explanation
1	A	When forming a fraction, the numerator will be the part of the whole and the denominator will be the whole or all parts together. In this case, there is 1 shaded part (the part) and there are 2 total parts (the whole). The fraction should be 1/2.
2	B	When forming a fraction, the numerator will be the part of the whole and the denominator will be the whole or all parts together. In this case, there is 1 shaded part (the part) and there are 4 total parts (the whole). The fraction should be 1/4.
3	D	When forming a fraction, the numerator will be the part of the whole and the denominator will be the whole or all parts together. In this case, there are 3 NOT shaded parts (the part) and there are 4 total parts (the whole). The fraction should be 3/4.

	Figure	Fraction
A		$\dfrac{1}{8}$
B		$\dfrac{1}{5}$
C		$\dfrac{1}{2}$

4

The correct answers are $\frac{1}{8}$, $\frac{1}{5}$, and $\frac{1}{2}$. Figure A is divided into 8 equal parts. 1 of the 8 parts represents $\frac{1}{8}$ of the whole figure. Figure B is divided into 5 equal parts. 1 of the 5 parts represents $\frac{1}{5}$ of the whole figure. Figure C is divided into 2 equal parts. 1 of the 2 parts represents $\frac{1}{2}$ of the whole figure.

Question No.	Answer	Detailed Explanation
5	C	Sad is the best answer choice to use in the blank. Marina likes spending time with her grandmother but had never spent more than one night away from her parents. Marina tells the reader that she is not happy. The opening line tells us Marina is going on the trip so she isn't confused. She is sad not concerned at the thought of not seeing her parents for two weeks.
6	A	The word choice, different, is correct. The second paragraph tells what the boy did that was not the same as last year.

Question No.	Answer	Detailed Explanation
7	B	Ferocious is the correct word that goes in the blank. It goes along with the detail that the author uses to describe the father dragon, "destroy things and fire-breather."
8	B	Rewarding is the best word choice for this title. Since a teacher is giving information to students it should be factual and relevant to the audience. The other three choices are more negative and if that was the case, why give the speech.

Week 8

Question No.	Answer	Detailed Explanation
1	B	The number line is divided into eight segments and the dot is at the sixth segment of the eight. The fraction is 6/8.
2	A	The number line is divided into six segments and the dot is at the first segment of the six. The fraction is 1/6.
3	C	The number line is divided into three segments and the dot is at the first segment of the three. The fraction is 1/3.
4		The interval from 0 to 1 is taken as the whole and is divided into 7 equal segments. Each segment has a size $\frac{1}{7}$. $\frac{5}{7}$ is represented by the Red dot located at the end of the 5th segment from 0 as shown in the figure below.

Question No.	Answer	Detailed Explanation
5	B	This answer choice is correct because the term "killer" as used in the sentence means something is "excellent".
6	A	This answer choice is correct because the term "out of touch" means "clueless". The other answer choices do not accurately explain "out of touch".
7	C	This answer choice is correct because the term "it's in the bag" can be correctly defined as "having been solved or completed".
8	D	This answer choice is correct because if 'something is grungy' then it is dirty. This answer choice accurately portrays this thought in a sentence. The other choices do not portray it in this manner.

Day 5

Question No.	Answer	Detailed Explanation
1	B	In order for a fraction to be between 0 and 3/4, it would have to be less than 3/4. Option B is the only choice that fits this criteria. (Note: 4/8 is equivalent to 1/2)
2	A	When comparing fractions, if the denominators are the same, compare the numerators to see which one is the smallest.
3	A	The answer has to be less than 1/2. Option A is the only choice that fits this criteria. 1/4 is less than 1/2, since fourths are smaller parts of a whole than halves. 4/8 is equal to 1/2, and 3/4 is greater.
4	D	In this problem, we are comparing the fractions with the same denominators. The numerators (the numerator represents the whole) in the fractions are different, and they are divided into the same number of equal parts (represented by the denominator). Therefore, the fraction with the greater numerator is greater than the fraction with the smaller numerator. So, $\frac{6}{7} > \frac{5}{7}$ (other three fractions $\frac{1}{7}$, $\frac{2}{7}$ and $\frac{4}{7}$ are less than $\frac{5}{7}$.)
5	A	Noonafter is not a time of day. Dawn refers to the early morning. The word aftermoon is misspelled incorrectly. The correct answer choice is afternoon.
6	C	The trunk of the tree, is not going to be wide. The obvious answer is that it is "not so wide". If it were really tiny, their feet would not fit on it.
7	A	Amy is clinging, and clearly there is fear. Frightened means afraid.
8	hard working	If she is a "diligent" worker that wants to make straight A's, this clearly relates to her being a hard worker. Hard workers strive for great success. The meanings "bored" and "fast" do not match her desire for straight A's, Clearly, she is not lazy if she strives for straight A's.

Week 9

Question No.	Answer	Detailed Explanation
1	A	The hour hand (the shorter hand) is past the 12th hour but has not reached the 1st hour, and the minute hand (the longer hand) is past 35 minutes but has not yet quite reached 40 minutes.
2	B	On a clock, the shorter hand points toward the hour and the longer hand points toward the minutes. For example, if it was 2:00, the shorter hand would point to the "2."
3	A	On a clock, the shorter hand points toward the hour and the longer hand points toward the minutes. For example, if it was 2:30, the longer hand would point to the "6," which represents the 30th minutes.
4		To determine what time John finishes his work, add 40 minutes to 5:30 PM; 5:30 PM + 40 minutes = 6:10 PM. This is represented on the number line below. 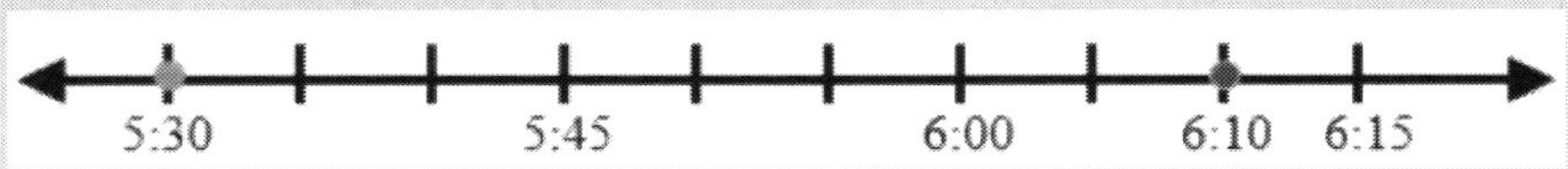 In the figure, green dot shows the time when John started the work, and the red dot shows the time when John finished his work.
5	A	Given that "wail" is the root word and "ed" is the suffix indicating past tense, the prefix is "be".
6	B	Let's look at the parts of the word in "telescope", there is the prefix "tele" and the root word "scope". The prefix "tele" means over a long distance, and "scope" refers to seeing. A telescope is a device that allows us to get a closer view of objects that are far away from us.
7	A	A suffix is found at the end of a word, and some answer choices can be quickly omitted. Also, "treat" is the root word. This leaves "ment" as the suffix.
8		The prefix is 'Dis'; The root word is 'agree' and 'able' is the suffix.

Day 2

Question No.	Answer	Detailed Explanation
1	B	From 4:00 to 5:00 is one hour of elapsed time. From 5:00 until 5:27 is an additional 27 minutes, for a total elapsed time of 1 hour and 27 minutes.
2	C	From 6:12 to 7:12 is 1 hour of elapsed time. From 7:12 to 7:15 is an additional 3 minutes, for a total elapsed time of 1 hour and 3 minutes.
3	D	From 7:06 to 8:06 is one hour of elapsed time. From 8:06 to 8:13 is an additional 7 minutes, for a total elapsed time of 1 hour and 7 minutes.
4	30 minutes	The time is 1 o'clock in the first picture. The time is 1:30 the second picture. 30 minutes have elapsed.
5	B	The definition states "to involve completely: ENGROSS" This closely matches "wrapped up" as used in the sentence.
6	B	The definition states "not before known, heard, or seen : UNFAMILIAR" is how the word strange was used in the given sentence. The other definitions do not apply.
7	C	This question asked about the measurement of time. The only word found in the glossary that was about time was A.M. Times between 12:00 (midnight) and 12:00 (noon).
8	C	This answer choice specifically answers the question (4 : to visualize or interpret as)

Question No.	Answer	Detailed Explanation
1	B	Options A and C would not be used to measure weight. Option D would be too small to measure the weight of a table. Option B is the most logical choice.
2	A	Capacity is another word for volume. Options B, C, and D would not be used to measure volume. Option A is the most logical choice.
3	C	Option A is a measure for volume. Option B is a measure of distance or length. Option D is a measure of temperature. Option C is the most logical choice.
4	Tea-spoon	From the given options, Teaspoon is the only tool used to measure small amounts of substances such as sugar.
5	A	The words that rhyme are "toil, soil, and boil"
6	B	Maria is waiting for the concert, to began and it makes sense that she would be a bit "uneasy". Happily, easily, and unfriendly are not correct.
7	C	An antonym is a word that has an opposite meaning from another. Laughed refers to positive, happy emotions, and "giggled" is a synonym. "Cried" is the antonym for the underlined word.
8	carelessly	Notice that the word carefully ends in the prefix -ful meaning that it is "full of care". On the other hand, carelessly ends in the prefix -less, meaning that there is no care. Clearly, these words are opposites or antonyms.

Day 4

Question No.	Answer	Detailed Explanation
1	C	First, add the totals number of students who chose Science and Math. 3 + 4 = 7. The chart states that each object stands for 2 votes. Multiply the Science and Math total by 2. 7 x 2 = 14.
2	C	The tallest bar indicates the food that was chosen most often. That would be considered the "favorite."
3	D	The foods with the shortest bars represent the foods that were least liked by the kids. Both salads and wraps had the least amount of votes.
4		Every fifth mark is drawn across the previous four marks.

In the tally of penny coins, there are four 5s (making it 4 x 5 = 20) and two singles (2 x 1 = 2). So, there are 22 pennies. Similarly, we can find that there are 18 nickels, 14 dimes and 16 quarters. |

Coins in John's Piggy Bank

Coin	Tally	Number of Coins
Penny	ⅢⅠ ⅢⅠ ⅢⅠ ⅢⅠ Ⅱ	22
Nickel	ⅢⅠ ⅢⅠ ⅢⅠ Ⅲ	18
Dime	ⅢⅠ ⅢⅠ Ⅲ	14
Quarter	ⅢⅠ ⅢⅠ ⅢⅠ Ⅰ	16

Tally chart is used to draw the bar graph given below.

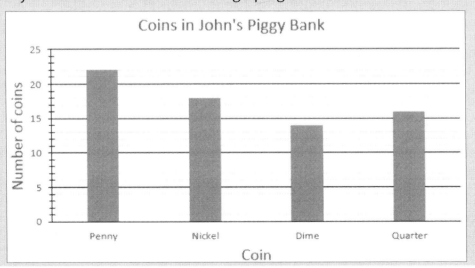

Question No.	Answer	Detailed Explanation
5	C	"Cloudy" correctly finishes the analogy.
6	A	This answer choice is correct because "tasty" can be substituted for "rich with flavor". The other answer choices would change the meaning of the sentence.
7	D	This answer choice is correct because "hilarious" can be substituted for "very funny". The other answer choices would change the meaning of the sentence.
8	C	This answer choice is correct because "smile" means the opposite of "snarl". The other answer choices mean something similar to "snarl".

Question No.	Answer	Detailed Explanation
1	C	Kilometers and meters are used to measure longer lengths. Grams are used to measure mass. Option C is the most appropriate.
2	A	Feet, yards, and miles are all used to measure longer lengths. The length of a pencil would be measured in inches.
3	A	Options B, C, and D are all too long to be the measure of a football. Option A is the most appropriate.

4

Measurement in inches	Measurement in half inches	Measurement in quarter inches
$2\frac{1}{2}$ inches	**5 half inches**	**10 quarter inches**
$5\frac{1}{2}$ inches	11 half inches	**22 quarter inches**
$6\frac{1}{2}$ inches	**13 half inches**	26 quarter inches

(1) 1 inch = 2 half inches; $2\frac{1}{2}$ inches = 2 inches + $\frac{1}{2}$ inch = 2 x 2 half inches + 1 half inch = 4 half inches + 1 half inch = 5 half inches.

1 half inch = 2 quarter inches. $2\frac{1}{2}$ inches = 5 half inches = 5 x 2 quarter inches = 10 quarter inches.

(2) 11 half inches = 10 half inches + 1 half inch = (10 ÷ 2) inches + $\frac{1}{2}$ inch = 5 inches + $\frac{1}{2}$ inch = $5\frac{1}{2}$ inches.

11 half inches = 11 x 2 quarter inches = 22 quarter inches.

(3) 26 quarter inches = 26 ÷ 2 half inches = 13 half inches.
13 half inches = 12 half inches + 1 half inch = (12 ÷ 2) inches + $\frac{1}{2}$ inch = 6 inches + $\frac{1}{2}$ inch = $6\frac{1}{2}$ inches.

Question No.	Answer	Detailed Explanation
5	C	This answer choice is correct because "enraged" replaces "infuriated" in the sentence without changing the meaning of the sentence. The other options all change the meaning of the original sentence.
6	A	"Enormous" replaces "tremendous" in the sentence without changing the meaning of the sentence.
7	D	This answer choice that is the most extreme is "overjoyed". The other answer choices cheerful, happy, and delighted are not as extreme.
8	D	This answer choice is correct because "behaved" is least like "naughty". The other options are similar to "naughty"

Day 6

Question No.	Answer	Detailed Explanation
1	C	If each box is a square unit, count the number of shaded boxes to get the area of the shaded region. There are 11 shaded boxes so the area is equal to 11 square units.
2	D	If each box is a square unit, count the number of boxes to get the area. There are 16 boxes so the area is equal to 16 square units.
3	C	If each box is a square unit, count the number of boxes to get the area. There are 24 boxes so the area is equal to 24 square units.
4	A & B	Each box is one square unit. Count the total number of square units in order to find the area. Another method is to count the square units along the width and multiply the total by the number of square units along the length.
5	B	The question defines the word "denominator."
6	D	The class that you would most likely learn about "mammals" is science class.
7	A	This answer is correct because the "sequence of events" of a story is the order in which events occur in the story.
8		If a teacher asks you to justify your answer, the teacher wants you to give proof of your answer.

STOP! IN THE NAME OF EDUCATION: PREVENT SUMMER LEARNING LOSS WITH 7 SIMPLE STEPS

Summer Learning loss is defined as "a loss of knowledge and skills . . . most commonly due to . . . . extended breaks [during the summertime] " (from edglossary.org/learning-loss). Many teachers have certainly had the experience of taking the first month of school not only to introduce his or her rules and procedures to the class but also to get the kids back "up to speed" with thinking, remembering what they've learned . . . and in many cases, reviewing previous content. With a traditional school calendar, then, this can mean that up to 10% of the school year is spent playing catch-up.

What's a parent to do? Fortunately, there are some simple steps you can take with your child to help your son or daughter both enjoy the summer and keep those all-important skills honed and fresh:

(1) Read!

Research supports the relationship between independent reading and student achievement, so simply having your child read daily will make a positive difference. Check out the following sources to find books that your child will want to dive into: your public library, local bookstores, online stores (Amazon, Barnes and Noble, half.com, etc.), and yard sales (if the family hosting the sale has children a bit older than your own, you stand a good chance of scoring discarded books that are a perfect match for your son or daughter's reading level).

(2) Write!

Have your child write letters to out-of-town friends and family, or write postcards while on vacation. A summer journal is another way to document summer activities. For the artistic or tech-savvy child, you may choose to create a family scrapbook with captions (consider the online options at Shutterfly, Mixbook, and Smilebox). Not only will you preserve this summer's memories, but your child will also continue to practice his or her writing skills! (See Summer is Here! Ideas to Keep Your Child's Writing Skills Sharp for more writing ideas.)

(3) Do the Math!

Think of ways your child can incorporate math skills into daily activities: have a yard sale, and put your child in charge of the cash box; help younger ones organize a lemonade stand (to practice salesmanship and making change). Or simply purchase a set of inexpensive flash cards to practice basic facts while waiting in line or on a long car ride. There's even a host of free online games that will keep your child's math skills sharp.

(4) "Homeschool" Your Child

Keeping your child's skills fresh doesn't have to cost a fortune: check out some of the Lumos Learning workbooks and online resources (at lumoslearning.com/store), and your child can work through several exercises each day. Even as little as twenty minutes a day can yield positive results, and it's easy to work in a small block of time here and there. For instance, your child can work in the book during a car ride, right before bedtime, etc. Or, simply make this part of your child's morning routine. For example: wake up, eat breakfast, complete chores, and then work in the workbook for 20 minutes. With time, you can make this a natural habit.

(5) Go Back-to-School Shopping (For a Great Summer School Learning Experience)

Check out offerings from the big names (think Sylvan, Huntington, Mathnasium, and Kumon), and also consider local summer schools. Some school districts and local colleges provide learning programs: research the offerings on-line for more information regarding the available options in your area.

(6) Take a Hike . . . Go Camping!

But "camp" doesn't always involve pitching a tent in the great outdoors. Nowadays, there are camps for every interest: sports camps, art camp, music camp, science camp, writing camp . . . the possibilities are endless! With a quick Internet search, you'll be able to turn up multiple options that will appeal to your son or daughter. And even if these camps aren't "academic", the life skills and interpersonal experiences are certain to help your child succeed in the "real world". For example, working together as a cast to put on a summer theater production involves memorizing lines, cooperation, stage crew coordination, and commitment – all skills that can come in handy when it comes to fostering a good work ethic and the ability to collaborate with others.

(7) Get tutored

Many teachers offer tutoring services throughout the summer months, either for individuals or small groups of students. Even the most school-averse student tends to enjoy the personal attention of a former teacher in a setting outside of the classroom. Plus, a tutor can tailor his or her instruction to pinpoint your child's needs – so you can maximize the tutoring sessions with the skills and concepts your child needs the most help with.

Of course, you don't need to do all seven steps to ensure that your child maintains his or her skills. Just following through with one or two of these options will go a long way toward continued learning, skills maintenance, and easing the transition to school when summer draws to a close.

SUMMER READING: QUESTIONS TO ASK THAT PROMOTE COMPREHENSION

As mentioned in our "Beating Summer Academic Loss" article, students are at risk of losing academic ground during the summer months, especially with respect to their reading level, spelling, and vocabulary. One of the best ways to prevent this "brain drain" for literacy is to have your son or daughter read each day during the summer break.

Better yet, you can promote these all-important skills and participate in your child's summer reading by engaging in active dialogue with your son or daughter. Below are several questions and ideas for discussion that will promote comprehension, recall, and critical thinking skills. In addition, these questions reflect several of the Common Core standards – which underpin the curriculum, instruction and standardized testing for most school districts. Of course, the standards vary by grade level, but some of the common themes that emerge in these standards are: citing evidence, summarizing, and making inferences.

• Citing evidence

Simply put, citing evidence involves going back into the text (book, magazine, newspaper, etc.) and finding "proof" to back up an answer, opinion, or assertion. For instance, you could ask your child, "Did you enjoy this book?" and then follow up that "yes" or "no" response with a "Why?" This requires the reader to provide details and examples from the story to support his or her opinion. For this particular question, then, your child may highlight plot events he or she liked, character attributes, writing style, and even genre (type of book) as evidence. Challenge for older students: Ask your child to go back into the text and find a direct quote to support an opinion or answer.

• Summarizing

For nonfiction pieces, this may involve being able to explain the 5W's – who, what, where, when, why (and how). For literature, ask your child to summarize the story elements, including: the setting, characters, main conflict or problem, events, resolution, and theme/lesson/moral. If your child can do this with specificity and accuracy, there's a very good chance that he or she comprehended the story. Challenge for older students: Ask your child to identify more complex story elements, such as the climax, rising action, and falling action.

• Making inferences

Making an inference is commonly referred to as "reading between the lines." That is, the reader can't find the answer to a question directly in the text but instead must synthesize or analyze information to come to a conclusion. To enhance these higher-level thinking skills, ask your child to describe the main character's personality, describe how a character changed by the end of a novel, or detail how the setting influenced the story's plot. Challenge for older students: Have the reader compare and contrast two or more characters to highlight similarities and differences in personality, actions, etc.

 Of course, if you read the same book that your child reads, you'll be able to come up with even more detailed questions – and also know if your child truly understood the reading based on his or her answers! But even if you don't get a chance to read what your child does, simply asking some of these questions not only helps your child's reading skills but also demonstrates an interest in your child – and his or her reading.

BEATING THE BRAIN DRAIN THROUGH LITERACY: WEBINAR RECAP WITH PRINTABLE ACTIVITY SHEET

Lumos Learning conducted webinar on "Beating the Brain Drain Through Literacy." During this webinar, we provided the students with several ideas for keeping their literacy skills sharp in the summertime.

Here's a handy chart with the ideas from the webinar, ready for you to post on your refrigerator. Let your child pick and choose the activities that appeal to him or her. Of course, reading should be nonnegotiable, but the list below provides alternatives for reluctant readers — or for those who just don't enjoy reading a traditional fiction novel. The first set of activities touch upon ideas that reinforce writing skills, while the second half addresses reading skills. There is also room on the chart to date or check off activities your child has completed.

Skill Area	Activity	Completed this activity	Notes for parents
Writing skills, spelling, and/or vocabulary	Keep a journal (things you do, places you go, people you meet)		Even though journals work on spelling skills, be sure your child understands that spelling "doesn't count". Most children like to keep their journals private, so they don't need to worry about perfect skills or that someone else is going to read/grade what they wrote.
	Start a blog		Enable privacy settings to keep viewers limited to friends and family. Check out WordPress, Squarespace, and Quillpad to begin blogging.
	Get published		The following places publish student work: The Clairmont Review, CyberKids, Creative Kids Magazine, New Moon, and The Young Writer's Magazine.
	Write letters		Have your child write or type letters, postcards, and emails to friends and family members.
	Take part in a family movie night		Watch movies that are thought-provoking to elicit interesting post-movie discussions. Other good bets are movies that are based on a book (read the book first and compare the two).
	Organize a family game night		Choose word games to work on spelling and vocabulary skills (examples: Scrabble, Boggle, and Hangman).
Reading skills: fluency, comprehension, critical thinking, decoding skills,inferencing, etc.	Pick up a good book!		Places to find/buy/borrow books include: your public library, ebooks, yard sales, book stores, your child's school library (if it's open during the summer), and borrowed books from friends and family members.
	Read materials that aren't "books"…		Ideas include: karaoke lyrics, cereal boxes, newspapers, magazines for kids, billboards, close captioning, and audio books.
	Compete! Enter a reading challenge		Scholastic Reading hosts a competition called "Reading Under the Stars" to break a world record for minutes read. Barnes and Noble gives students the opportunity to earn one free book with "Imagination's Destination" reading challenge.

Note: Reading just six books over the summer can maintain – and sometimes even increase! – your child's reading level. Not sure if the book is appropriate for your child's reading level? Use the five-finger rule: have your son/daughter read a page of a book. Each time your child encounters a word that is unfamiliar or unknown, he or she holds up a finger. If your child holds up more than five fingers on a given page, that book is probably too difficult.

However, there are some books that a child will successfully tackle if it's high-interest to him or her. Keep in mind that reading levels are a guide (as is the five-finger rule), and some children may exceed expectations…so don't hold your child back if he or she really wants to read a particular book (even if it may appear to be too challenging).

Remember, if students do some of these simple activities, they can prevent the typical four to six weeks of learning loss due to the "summer slide." And since spelling, vocabulary and reading skills are vulnerable areas, be sure to encourage your child to maintain his or her current literacy level…it will go a long way come September!

SUMMER IS HERE! KEEP YOUR CHILD'S WRITING SKILLS SHARP WITH ONLINE GAMES

Like Reading and math, free online activities exist for all subjects… and writing is no exception. Check out the following free interactive writing activities, puzzles, quizzes and games that reinforce writing skills and encourage creativity:

Primary Level (K-2nd Grade)

Story Writing Game

In this game, the child fills in the blanks of a short story. The challenge is for the storyteller to choose words that fit the kind of story that has been selected. For example, if the child chooses to tell a ghost story, then he or she must select words for each blank that would be appropriate for a scary tale. http://www.funenglishgames.com/writinggames/story.html

Opinions Quiz for Critical Thinking

Practice developing logical reasons to support a thesis with this interactive activity. Students read the stated opinion, such as, "We should have longer recess because…" The child must then select all of the possible reasons from a list that would support the given statement. The challenge lies with the fact that each statement may have more than one possible answer, and to receive credit, the student must select all correct responses. This game is best suited for older primary students. http://www. netrover.com/~kingskid/Opinion/opinion.html

Interactives: Sequence

Allow your child to practice ordering events with this interactive version of the fairy tale, Cinderella. The child looks at several pictures from the story and must drag them to the bottom of the screen to put the events in chronological order. When the player mouses over each scene from the story, a sentence describing the image appears and is read aloud to the student. Once the events are in order, the student can learn more about the plot and other story elements with the accompanying tutorials and lessons. http://www.learner.org/interactives/story/sequence.html

WEBINAR "CLIFF NOTES" FOR BEATING SUMMER ACADEMIC LOSS: AN INFORMATIVE GUIDE TO PARENTS

The "Summer Slide"

First, it's important to understand the implications of "summer slide" – otherwise known as summer learning loss. Research has shown that some students who take standardized tests in the fall could have lost up to 4-6 weeks of learning each school year (when compared with test results from the previous spring). This means that teachers end up dedicating the first month of each new school year for reviewing material before they can move onto any new content and concepts.

The three areas that suffer most from summer learning loss are in the areas of vocabulary/reading, spelling, and math. In Stop! In the Name of Education: Prevent Summer Learning Loss With 7 Simple Steps, we discussed some activities parents could use with children to prevent summer slide. Let's add to that list with even more ways to keep children engaged and learning – all summer long.

Be sure to check out:

• Your Child's School

Talk to child's teacher, and tell him or her that you'd like to work on your child's academics over the summer. Most teachers will have many suggestions for you.

In addition to the classroom teacher as a resource, talk to the front office staff and guidance counselors. Reading lists and summer programs that are organized through the school district may be available for your family, and these staff members can usually point you in the right direction.

• Your Community

A quick Google search for "free activities for kids in (insert your town's name)" will yield results of possible educational experiences and opportunities in your area. Some towns offer "dollar days", park lunches, and local arts and entertainment.

You may even wish to involve your child in the research process to find fun, affordable memberships and discounts to use at area attractions. For New Jerseyans and Coloradans, check out www.funnewjersey.com and www.colorado.com for ideas.

Of course, don't forget your local library! In addition to books, you can borrow movies and audiobooks, check out the latest issue of your favorite magazine, and get free Internet access on the library's computers. Most libraries offer a plethora of other educational choices, too – from book clubs and author visits to movie nights and crafts classes, you're sure to find something at your local branch that your child will enjoy.

• Stores

This is an extremely engaging activity – and your child won't even know he or she is learning! For grocery shopping, ask your child to write the list while you dictate. At the store, your son/daughter can locate the items and keep a cost tally to stay within a specified budget. At the checkout, you can have a contest to see whose estimate of the final bill is most accurate – and then reward the winner!

You may wish to plan a home improvement project or plant a garden: for this, your child can make the list, research the necessary materials, and then plan and execute the project after a visit to your local home improvement store. All of these activities involve those three critical areas of spelling, vocabulary/reading, and math.

• The Kitchen

This is one of the best places to try new things – by researching new foods, recipes, and discussing healthy food choices – while practicing math skills (such as measuring ingredients, doubling recipes, etc.). Your child may also enjoy reading about new cultures and ethnicities and then trying out some new menu items from those cultures.

• The Television

TV doesn't have to be mind numbing … when used appropriately. You can watch sports with your child to review stats and make predictions; watch documentaries; or tune into the History Channel, Discovery, National Geographic, HGTV, and more. Anything that teaches, helps your child discover new interests, and promotes learning new things together is fair game.

As an extension, you may decide to research whether or not the show portrays accurate information. And for those children who really get "into" a certain topic, you can enrich their learning by taking related trips to the museum, doing Internet research, and checking out books from the library that tie into the topic of interest.

• Movies

Movies can be educational, too, if you debrief with your child afterwards. Schedule a family movie night, and then discuss how realistic the movie was, what the messages were, etc.

For book-based movies (such as Judy Moody, Harry Potter, Percy Jackson, etc.), you could read the book together first, and then view the movie version. Comparing and contrasting the two is another terrific educational way to enjoy time together and work on your child's reasoning skills.

Note: www.imdb.com and www.commonsensemedia.org are great sites for movie recommendations and movie reviews for kids and families.

• Games

Playing games promotes taking turns, reading and math skills, and strategy development. Scour yard sales for affordable board games like Scrabble, Monopoly, Uno, Battleship, and Qwirkle.

Don't forget about non-board games, like those found on the Wii, Nintendo, Xbox, and other gaming consoles. You'll still want to choose wisely and limit your child's screen time, but these electronic versions of popular (and new) games mirror the way kids think … while focusing on reading and math skills. For more ideas, Google "education apps" for suggestions.

•Books, books, books!

Of course, nothing beats reading for maintaining skills. When you can connect your child with a book that is of interest to him or her, it can be fun for your child, build confidence, and improve fluency.

To help your child find a book that's "just right", use the five-finger rule: choose a page from a possible book and have your child read that page. Every time he or she encounters an unknown word, put up a finger. If your child exceeds five fingers (that is, five unknown words), that book is probably too challenging and he or she may wish to pass on it.

For reluctant readers, consider non-book reading options, like:magazines (such as Ranger Rick, American Girl, Discovery Kids, and Sports Illustrated for Kids), cereal boxes, billboards, current events, closed captioning, and karaoke. If you keep your eyes open, you'll find there are many natural reading opportunities that surround us every day.

Whatever you do, remember to keep it fun. Summer is a time for rest and rejuvenation, and learning doesn't always have to be scheduled. In fact, some of the most educational experiences are unplanned.

Visit lumoslearning.com/parents/summer-program for more information.

Valuable Learning Experiences: A Summer Activity Guide for Parents

Soon school will be out of session, leaving the summer free for adventure and relaxation. However, it's important to also use the summer for learning activities. Giving your son or daughter opportunities to keep learning can result in more maturity, self-growth, curiosity, and intelligence. Read on to learn some ways to make the most of this summer.

Read

Summer is the perfect time to get some extra reading accomplished. Youth can explore books about history, art, animals, and other interests, or they can read classic novels that have influenced people for decades. A lot of libraries have summer fun reading programs which give children, teens, and adults little weekly prizes for reading books. You can also offer a reward, like a $25 gift card, if your child reads a certain amount of books.

Travel

"The World is a book and those who do not travel read only a page." This quote by Saint Augustine illustrates why travel is so important for a student (and even you!). Travel opens our eyes to new cultures, experiences, and challenges. When you travel, you see commonalities and differences between cultures.

Professor Adam Galinsky of Columbia Business School, who has researched travel benefits, said in a Quartz article that travel can help a child develop compassion and empathy: "Engaging with another culture helps kids recognize that their own egocentric way of looking at the world is not the only way of being in the world."

If the student in your life constantly complains about not having the newest iPhone, how would they feel seeing a child in a third-world country with few possessions? If you child is disrespectful and self-centered, what would they learn going to Japan and seeing a culture that promotes respect and otherness instead of self-centeredness?

If you can't afford to travel to another country, start a family travel fund everyone can contribute to and in the meantime, travel somewhere new locally! Many people stay in the area they live instead of exploring. Research attractions in your state and nearby states to plan a short road trip to fun and educational places!

Visit Museums

You can always take your children to visit museums. Spending some quality time at a museum can enhance curiosity because children can learn new things, explore their interests, or see exhibits expanding upon school subjects they recently studied. Many museums have seasonal exhibits, so research special exhibits nearby. For example, "Titanic: The Artifact Exhibition" has been making its way to various museums in the United States. It contains items recovered from the Titanic as well as interactive activities and displays explaining the doomed ship's history and tragic demise. This year, the exhibit is visiting Las Vegas, Orlando, and Waco.

Work

A final learning suggestion for the summer is for students to get a job, internship, or volunteer position. Such jobs can help with exploring career options. For example, if your child is thinking of becoming a vet, they could walk dogs for neighbors, or if your child wants to start their own business, summer is the perfect time to make and sell products.

Not only will a job or volunteer work look good on college applications, but it will also teach your children valuable life lessons that can result in more maturity and responsibility. You could enhance the experience by teaching them accounting and illustrating real world problems to them, like budgeting money for savings and bills.

The above suggestions are just four of the many ways you can help learning continue for your child or children all summer long. Experience and seeing things first-hand are some of the most important ways that students can learn, so we hope you find the above suggestions helpful in designing a fun, educational, and rewarding summer that will have benefits in and out of the classroom.

Additional Information

What if I buy more than one Lumos Study Program?

Step 1

Visit the URL and login to your account.
http://www.lumoslearning.com

Step 2

Click on 'My tedBooks' under the "Account" tab.
Place the Book Access Code and submit.

Step 3

To add the new book for a registered student, choose the
● Existing Student button and select the student and submit.

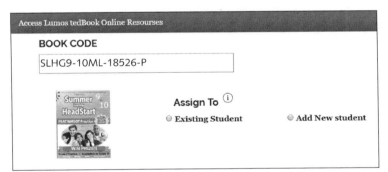

To add the new book for a new student, choose the ● Add New student
button and complete the student registration.

Lumos tedBooks for State Assessments Practice

Lumos tedBook for standardized test practice provides necessary grade-specific state assessment practice and skills mastery. Each tedBook includes hundreds of standards-aligned practice questions and online summative assessments that mirror actual state tests.

The workbook provides students access to thousands of valuable learning resources such as worksheets, videos, apps, books, and much more.

Lumos Learning tedBooks for State Assessment	
SBAC Math & ELA Practice Book	CA, CT, DE, HI, ID, ME, MI, MN, NV, ND, OR, WA, WI
NJSLA Math & ELA Practice Book	NJ
ACT Aspire Math & ELA Practice Book	AL, AR
IAR Math & ELA Practice Book	IL
FSA Math & ELA Practice Book	FL
PARCC Math & ELA Practice Book	DC, NM
GMAS Math & ELA Practice Book	GA
NYST Math & ELA Practice Book	NY
ILEARN Math & ELA Practice Book	IN
LEAP Math & ELA Practice Book	LA
MAP Math & ELA Practice Book	MO
MAAP Math & ELA Practice Book	MS
AZM2 Math & ELA Practice Book	AZ
MCAP Math & ELA Practice Book	MD
OST Math & ELA Practice Book	OH
MCAS Math & ELA Practice Book	MA
CMAS Math & ELA Practice Book	CO
TN Ready Math & ELA Practice Book	TN
STAAR Math & ELA Practice Book	TX
NMMSSA Math & ELA Practice Book	NM

Available

- At Leading book stores
- www.lumoslearning.com/a/lumostedbooks

Made in the USA
Monee, IL
17 June 2022

9817458 3R00140